Energy Coverage — Media Panic

Longman Series in Public Communication
Series Editor: Ray Eldon Hiebert

Energy Coverage–Media Panic

AN INTERNATIONAL PERSPECTIVE

The Media Institute

Edited by
Nelson Smith
Leonard J. Theberge

Longman
New York & London

Energy Coverage — Media Panic
An International Perspective

Longman Inc., 1560 Broadway, New York, N.Y. 10036
Associated companies, branches, and representatives
throughout the world.

Developmental Editor: Gordon T. R. Anderson
Editorial and Design Supervisor: Diane Perlmuth
Production Supervisor: Ferne Y. Kawahara
Manufacturing Supervisor: Marion Hess

Library of Congress Cataloging in Publication Data
Main entry under title:
Energy coverage—media panic.
  (Longman series in public communication)
  Includes index.
  1. Petroleum industry and trade in the press—Ad-
dresses, essays, lectures. 2. Atomic power
industry in the press—Addresses, essays, lectures.
I. Theberge, Leonard J. II. Smith, Nelson,
1950-   . III. Media Institute (Washington, D.C.)
IV. Series.
PN4771.E53 1983 070.4'4933379   82-14810
ISBN 0-582-29018-X

Manufactured in the United States of America

This book is dedicated to J. Robert Fluor, a thoughtful man of great integrity, whose wise counsel and support over many years made it possible.

Contents

Preface

While visiting Great Britain in 1979 and again in 1980, I met with a number of Fleet Street's financial and business reporters and editors, and had a chance to discuss with them their approaches toward the coverage of business and economic issues. At the time, The Media Institute had initiated several studies of the content of American television network news in key areas of nuclear power, coal, and inflation.

I discovered that British journalists familiar with American business and economic news were impressed by much of the U.S. coverage. However, American television networks were often criticized for superficial or sensational reporting on one energy issue—the oil crises of the 1970s. A study completed by The Media Institute in 1982 supported this opinion, concluding that oil crisis coverage failed to give the viewing public sufficient information to make an informed judgment about causes or solutions. The Media Institute's study also found that networks generally ignored the real debate over market versus non-market forces, giving instead paramount attention to non-market solutions; and that the networks demonstrated an over-reliance on government sources for information about the causes of and solutions to the oil crises.

Energy was the great economic story of the 1970s. It was a phenomenon not confined to the United States but one which seriously affected the entire world. The oil crisis seemed to offer an excellent case history of press performance on economic issues. Certainly, from the American point of view, it showed some of the strengths and weaknesses of our press organizations in dealing with complex economic issues: strengths such as the technological and logistical capabilities to reach everywhere on the globe where energy news was being made; weaknesses such as the over-dramatization and oversimplification of complex economic developments.

With this background, The Media Institute assembled a distinguished group of journalists, academics, business leaders and government officials from the United States, France, West Germany, Great Britain, and Japan to meet at Ditchley Park, England (see p. xiii for listing and biographies of participants). The objective was to examine the role played by media reporting in the processes by which the various countries adapted to the oil crises of the 1970s. It was also decided that nuclear power was an energy story present-

ing a complex range of economic and technical issues which made it difficult
for journalists to report.

We obtained papers from Dr. Hans Mathias Kepplinger, professor of
communications, University of Mainz; Françoise Monier, senior energy/
environment correspondent, *L'Express* and Beatrice Lacoste, freelance
journalist in Paris; Alan Reynolds of Polyconomics, Inc.; and Norman
Macrae, deputy editor of *The Economist*. The essays examined the
coverage of oil and nuclear power as well the relationship between press institutions and energy policy in their respective countries. Sakae Nagaoka,
commentator for the Japan Broadcasting Company, delivered a paper on
media coverage of nuclear power in Japan; Charles Snow, senior editor of
the *Middle East Economic Survey* and a veteran observer of the political
and economic events in that region, presented a talk on the treatment of
OPEC in the Western media; and Nelson Smith, a writer and media consultant formerly with the Independent Petroleum Association of America,
served as conference coordinator and co-editor of this book. A conscious
effort was made to include differing perspectives from a variety of authors
and guests. The oil industry and Friends of the Earth were both
to be found on our panel, and the spectrum of opinion represented was wide
indeed.

The following chapters include the edited papers which formed the basis
of discussions at the conference. Following each group of papers is an
essay along with interesting sections of the conference transcript itself. It is
hoped the reader will find these proceedings as insightful and thought-
provoking as did the participants at Ditchley Park.

A few words about the structure and intent of the conference may be
useful. Our original goal was to provide a comprehensive cross-cultural
study of energy coverage by examining the response of the press in each of
these countries to what was essentially the same economic problem. In
drawing together the participants and materials for the conference, several
things became evident. First, the economic crisis itself was viewed and
treated differently from country to country. The economic effect of the
1973 oil embargo and subsequent price rise was mitigated in some cases
and exacerbated in others by media coverage and government policies. The
press played a key role in influencing how governments responded to the
difficulty. Dr. Kepplinger's paper demonstrates the extent to which the
German press influenced the climate for policymaking in the Federal
Republic of Germany. The Reynolds paper and the conference transcripts
show similar influences in other countries.

Second, the relationship between press and government differs from
country to country. News organizations in the United States exist in a
system of commercial competition and are protected by a broadly inter-
preted constitutional mandate of press freedom. In Great Britain, there are
similar but narrower legal safeguards for press freedom; however, the main

broadcasting system (British Broadcasting Corporation) has no commercial advertisements and is funded in part by the Treasury. The French print press is vigorously independent from the government, but the three television networks operate under direct and obvious government control (a situation which may be changing under President Mitterand). The West German print press is legally protected like that of the United States, and the broadcast media is a public/private hybrid organized much like the U.S. Public Broadcasting System. Therefore, analyzing the content of energy coverage in the context of these different media cultures is something like comparing apples with oranges. Add to that complexity the various factors contributing to the energy crisis, and the study of international energy reporting becomes a formidable task.

Our approach was to commission a comprehensive paper on the handling of a given problem in a particular country, and then to ask the participants at Ditchley Park for extended comment on the corresponding experiences of their own media and political institutions. The first session started with papers presented by Messrs. Reynolds and Kepplinger and dealt with coverage of oil issues. In the second session papers were presented by Mlles. Monier and Lacoste and Mr. Nagaoka which addressed the coverage of nuclear power. The final session was based upon Norman Macrae's paper on the British press which examined institutional tendencies in press organizations' approach to energy and economic coverage.

The result of this approach is a study of energy and economic coverage which transcends national limitations. While it is not and does not pretend to be a comprehensive analysis of energy coverage in all five nations, it is the first systematic attempt to put this coverage into the international perspective of five major industrialized nations. At the same time, we have also provided some bench marks against which to measure press coverage of business and economic activity.

The title of this book is *Energy Coverage—Media Panic*. While the former phrase is self-explanatory, there may be some puzzlement about our choice of the term "media panic" to describe energy coverage during the 1970s. In a state of panic, an individual's critical faculties are impaired. Time seems elongated, and there is an obsessive focus on the here and now. No amount of information or data can dislodge the sense of anxiety, and in an effort to placate a worried mind, the panic-stricken individual may look for an elaborate or contrived explanation for his problem. There is evidence that news organizations in the United States and abroad may have lost some part of their critical faculties in covering energy shortages. In the United States, for example, the media displayed an obsessive concentration on the "conspiracy theory," which posited that oil companies had contrived oil shortages in order to increase prices and profits. There were also many political figures who helped to promote the "conspiracy theory," which was very popular at the time of Watergate.

A classic example of "media panic" was the Three Mile Island accident. Before that event, the television networks had paid scant attention to nuclear power even though it represented a significant factor in American electrical energy use. The networks were simply unprepared to handle the technical complexity of the subject. Knowing little about nuclear energy, while knowing a great deal about how to cover a catastrophe, the networks portrayed the TMI accident in the terms of their training. The lack of technical knowledge among reporters inhibited their own critical faculties and the result, in organizational terms, was panic—a panic which was communicated to the public.

Our criticism of energy coverage is not universal. There were members of the press corps in each of the countries who did not succumb to panic and performed a solid job in covering this challenging issue. It is safe to say that most reporters attempted to tell the story accurately. But in many cases, the results of their collective efforts added up to less than the sum of the individual parts. It is for this reason that we decided to examine press institutions themselves to see whether there were structural, financial, or political explanations for the shortcomings we witnessed. As you will see from the following essays, "media panic" was mainly the result of un-prepared organizations, rather than malicious individuals.

The discussions and writings in this volume are remarkable in that they reflect common concerns, although their authors hail from six nations, three continents, and diverse backgrounds. While each nation is unique in its media-culture, political system, and press constraints, in the day-to-day gathering and reporting of information, reporters share ethical concerns and logistical difficulties which transcend national borders. It may be, for example, that the French television correspondent and his American counterpart have more in common, in terms of their daily routine, than do a broadcaster and print reporter in the United States. In the end, it may be that the unifying principle of reporting the news is the major factor determining coverage content in nations which have an independent press.

I would like to express my personal appreciation to the participants, sponsors, and organizers of the Ditchley Park conference, including the staffs of The Media Institute and Ditchley Park.

Leonard J. Theberge
President, The Media Institute

Washington, D.C.

Biographical Sketches of Participants

UNITED STATES

Tom Bethell DeWitt Wallace Chair of Communication, American Enterprise Institute for Public Policy Research, 1981-82. A graduate of Oxford, Mr. Bethell is a former editor of *Washington Monthly* and, most recently, Washington editor of *Harper's Magazine*. He is also the Washington correspondent for *The American Spectator*. Some of his *Harper's* articles have won awards, notably an article in the October 1979 issue which won first prize in the John Hancock Award and an "honorable mention" in the Gerald Loeb Award. Mr. Bethell has also studied and published works on the history of jazz, including a 1977 biography of the New Orleans jazz clarinetist, George Lewis.

Richard L. Dunham President, H. Zinder & Associates, a division of ZCI. Mr. Dunham served as chairman of the Federal Power Commission, 1975-77, and acted as administrator of the Emergency Natural Gas Act of 1977. A former deputy director of the White House Domestic Council, Mr. Dunham also served as director of the Budget for New York State. He was resident fellow at the American Enterprise Institute for Public Policy Research and has also served as president of Rochester Computer Services.

Dr. Robert L. DuPont Psychiatrist, president of Institute for Behavior and Health, Inc.; president of the nonprofit Phobia Society of America; and clinical professor of psychiatry at Georgetown University. Dr. DuPont is the author of The Media Institute study "Nuclear Phobia—Phobic Thinking About Nuclear Power."

Robert S. Goralski Director of Information, Gulf Oil Corporation, Washington, D.C. A newsman for 26 years, Mr. Goralski joined NBC News in Washington in 1961. He covered the State Department and the Pentagon, and was NBC News correspondent at the White House during the Kennedy and Johnson administrations. He has reported from the Middle East, Vietnam, the Dominican Republic, and other areas of crises in more than 40 countries. He has written numerous articles for magazines and newspapers, and is the author of the *Encyclopedia Britannica Yearbook* articles on Vietnam. Mr. Goralski is the author of *World War II Almanac*, a political and military record of the conflict published in 1981.

Jeff Greenfield Author and critic whose commentary on the media appears on CBS-TV's "Sunday Morning" program. Mr. Greenfield, a former speech-writer for Robert F. Kennedy, has written on politics and journalism for a number of publications. Recently, he acted as moderator of a panel discussion on CBS-TV's "60 Minutes" which examined the practices of that show itself. Mr. Greenfield's most recent book is *The Real Campaign: How the Media Missed the Story of the 1980 Campaign*.

David Kelley, Ph.D. Assistant professor of Philosophy, Vassar College. Dr. Kelley has taught at Vassar since 1975, and has written for a wide audience on a variety of topics. He has addressed the Mont Pelerin Society on the ethics of capitalism, commented on affirmative action for WNEW-TV in New York, and discussed media bias against business for the SmithKline Forum. He comments regularly on economic issues for the radio series "Perspective on the Economy," and has written extensively for *Barron's National Business & Financial Weekly*, and other publications on the media and the role of ideas in the marketplace. He is currently completing a book entitled *The Evidence of the Senses*.

John F. O'Leary President, O'Leary & Associates, Washington, D.C. Mr. O'Leary, an energy economist for 30 years, was the first deputy secretary of energy, assuming that post as of the creation of the Department of Energy in 1977. He served in that capacity for two years. Prior to that, he was administrator of the Federal Energy Administration. His experience includes terms as administrator of the New Mexico Energy Resources Board, director of licensing for the Atomic Energy Commission, and director of the Bureau of Mines. In private industry, Mr. O'Leary has been technical director of energy resources and the environment division of the MITRE Corporation, and a private consultant on energy matters to government agencies and the private sector.

Anthony J. Parisi Correspondent, *Petroleum Intelligence Weekly*. A trained engineer, Mr. Parisi has been writing on energy-related matters for a number of publications for more than a decade. Prior to joining *PIW*, he was an energy correspondent for the *New York Times*; prior to that, he was on the staff of *Business Week* magazine, serving for three years as energy editor. For his *Business Week* cover story, "Will Energy Conservation Throttle Economic Growth?," Mr. Parisi won first prize for general circulation magazines in the 1977 Business Journalism Awards given by the University of Michigan. He twice received a *New York Times* Publisher's Award for his energy coverage.

Roger Peterson   Energy correspondent, ABC News. Mr. Peterson's career with ABC goes back to 1962, when he joined the Chicago affiliate, WBKB-TV as a reporter, writer, and producer. In 1966 he became a full-time correspondent and joined the Saigon bureau. He served as ABC Tokyo Bureau Chief from December 1967 to October 1969, returning to the United States to become a national correspondent. In 1970 he covered the Pentagon, and in 1973 was assigned to Washington, with special emphasis on the emerging energy issue.

Dr. Claude G. Poncelet   Director, Issue Analysis & Management Department, Power Systems Company, Westinghouse Electric Corporation. Dr. Poncelet, who holds degrees in electrical engineering, nuclear engineering, and physics, has been associated with Westinghouse since 1960. From 1960 to 1967, he was with the Atomic Power division and became fellow scientist with responsibilities in nuclear power reactor design. He joined Carnegie-Mellon University in 1967, where he was professor of nuclear engineering, and, from 1969 to 1975, chairman of the Nuclear Science and Engineering Department. He left the University in 1975 to become scientific advisor in the Westinghouse Energy Action Office, becoming Director in 1980. He assumed his current position in 1981. Dr. Poncelet has over 70 publications in the fields of nuclear energy and energy systems.

Alan Reynolds   Vice-president and chief economist, Polyconomics, Inc., Morristown, New Jersey. Mr. Reynolds, formerly vice-president for Business and Economic Research, First National Bank of Chicago, is a member of the editorial boards of *National Review* and *The American Spectator*. He is a frequent contributor to these publications, the *Wall Street Journal*, and others.

Herbert Schmertz   Vice-president, Public Affairs, Mobil Oil Corporation. Mr. Schmertz, a director of Mobil Corporation, holds an LL.B. degree from Columbia University. A former general counsel and assistant to the director of the Federal Mediation and Conciliation Service, Mr. Schmertz joined Mobil in 1966 as manager of the corporate labor relations department. He was elected vice-president for Public Affairs in July, 1969, a position he has held since then except for a stint in 1973-74 as president of Mobil Shipping and Transportation Company. He is a director of the Municipal Art Society and a director of the International Council of the National Academy of Television Arts and Sciences; he is also a member of the Council on Foreign Relations. Mr. Schmertz is co-author of the novel, *Takeover*.

Nelson Smith   Writer and media consultant. Mr. Smith holds a B.S. in Foreign Service from Georgetown University; he has worked as a congressional press aide and as manager of media relations for the Independent Petroleum Association of America. During 1978 and 1979, Mr. Smith served as chairman of the Sub-committee on Alternative Fuels of the Republican National Committee Advisory Council on Natural Resources. He is currently director of public affairs at the Manhattan Institute for Policy Research in New York City.

William D. Smith   Senior media advisor, Exxon Corporation, Washington D.C. Mr. Smith was a reporter for the *New York Times* for 17 years, serving as chief energy correspondent from 1967–77. He is the winner of the Association of Petroleum Writers Award for Outstanding Journalistic Performance; the Notable Journalistic Achievement Award of the American Association of Petroleum Geologists; first prize in the A.T. Kearney Excellence in Business Reporting competition, and *New York Times* Publisher's Award. Mr. Smith was the first reporter on a general interest newspaper to cover OPEC. He is also the author of the book, *Northwest Passage—The Voyage of the S. S. Manhattan.*

James C. Tanner   Vice-president, International Publications, Petroleum Information Corporation. Formerly energy editor of the *Wall Street Journal*, Mr. Tanner joined Petroleum Information Corporation in 1981 as a vice-president in charge of the new International Publications Division. He is also serving as editor of *Petroleum Information International.*

Leonard J. Theberge   President, The Media Institute. Mr. Theberge was founder and president of the National Legal Center for the Public Interest; he served as international counsel for the Upjohn Company and as vice-president for Public Affairs of Rohr Industries. He holds an honour's degree in politics, philosophy and economics from the University of Oxford, and is currently chairman of the International Communications Committee, a subcommittee of the American Bar Association's Section of International Law.

GREAT BRITAIN

Tom Burke   Board of Directors, 1975–81, and director of Special Projects, Friends of the Earth, 1979–81. Mr. Burke was press officer of the European Environment Bureau, 1979, and press officer at Great George's Community Arts Project, 1969–70. He has lectured at West Cheshire College, 1970–71, and Old Swan Technical College, 1971–73, and was coordinator at Merseyside Friends of the Earth Ltd., 1973–75, and Director, 1975–79. Mr. Burke was a member of the Board of Directors, Earth Resources Research, 1975; Waste Management Advisory Council, 1976; and Packaging Council, 1978.

Alan T. Gregory   Director of British Petroleum International, Ltd. since 1975. Currently he is regional director for the United Kingdom and Ireland and is responsible for the BP Group's external afffairs. He is Director of BP Chemicals International Ltd., BP Exploration Ltd., and BP Nutrition Ltd. Mr. Gregory has been with BP since 1971. Prior to that, he was an administrative civil servant from 1948 to 1970 and worked in the Ministries of Power and Technology and the Department of Trade and Industry. During this period, he was the United Kingdom's representative on the OECD Oil Committee and Chairman of the NATO Petroleum Planning Committee.

Adrian Hamilton   Editor of the *Times* of London Business News since early 1981. Mr. Hamilton began his journalistic career on the *Los Angeles Times* working as a reporter and rewrite man, after gaining a degree at Oxford. He was features editor at *Vogue* before going to the *Financial Times*. He was the Times' energy editor for five years and, for two years, its industrial editor. He left the *Times* for the *Observer*, becoming editor of its business section. Mr. Hamilton has written three books, including two on oil: *Oil, the Biggest Business* and with C. Tugendhat, *Offshore Oil, the Impact of the North Sea on the British Economy*.

Sir John Hill   Chairman, UK Atomic Energy Authority, 1967–81; British Nuclear Fuels Ltd. since 1971; Amersham International PLC since 1975. Sir John joined UKAEA in 1959 (Member for Production 1964–67). He is a member of the Advisory Council on Technology (1968–70); the Nuclear Power Advisory Board since 1973, and the Energy Commission (1977–79).

Norman Macrae   Deputy editor, *The Economist* (London).

FRANCE

Michel Anfrol   Director of Special Events, TFI. Mr. Anfrol spent 14 years in the United States as a news correspondent.

Beatrice Lacoste   Free-lance journalist based in Paris researching and reporting on issues pertaining to energy and the environment. Ms. Lacoste represents the Sierra Club in France and is a correspondent for the monthly *Renewable Energy News*. In 1979–80 she covered seminars on the marine environment and related eco-systems in Asia and the Far East. From 1975–79 Ms. Lacoste traveled extensively in Latin America, the Caribbean, East Africa, and the Indian Ocean Islands, reporting on appropriate technology experiences and development problems. She has also toured the United States to write a story on the national parks and recreation system.

Françoise Monier Senior energy/environment correspondent, *L' Express*.

Jean Pellerin Director, Public Relations Department, Commissariat a l'Energie Atomique. Mr. Pellerin is a member of the boards of the Institut Français de l'Energie; the Societe Française d'Energie Nucleaire and the Revue Generale de l'Ectricite. Formerly, M. Pellerin was assistant director of the Physics Division and Biology Department of the CEA, and was attache in the National Audit Office (Cour des Comptes).

FEDERAL REPUBLIC OF GERMANY

Ulrich Daunert Scientific counsellor, Embassy of the Federal Republic of Germany, London.

Dr. Hans Mathias Kepplinger Professor of communications, Institut fur Publizistik, University of Mainz. Dr. Kepplinger has been affiliated at the Institut since 1970; his doctoral thesis has been published as a book entitled *Rechte Leute von links. Gewaltkult und Innerlichkeit*. He has, since 1976, been co-director of a study, "Community and Communication," still ongoing, which was designed in cooperation with UNESCO. He has presented papers at conferences in the United States, under the auspices of the American Association for Public Opinion, the International Communication Association and other bodies, and has been a research fellow at the University of California, Berkely. In 1979 he published *Creating a Crisis: German Mass Media and Oil Supply in 1973-74*.

Dr. Isabel Muhlfenzel Documentary producer, Bayerische Rundfunk.

Thomas Ukert Media relations manager, Esso A.G. Mr. Ukert joined Esso A.G.'s Public Affairs Department in 1951 as head of Photo Files and Services. Between 1953 and 1962 he was editor of the company's institutional magazine. Until the early 1970s, he worked as manager of creative services with responsibility for all publications and visual aids produced by Esso A.G.'s Public Affairs Department. Since 1973 he has been media relations manager.

JAPAN

Sakae Nagaoka News commentator, Japan Broadcasting Company. Mr. Nagaoka joined JBC's script department in 1950 and wrote radio drama scenarios. Since 1959 he produced scientific programs for both radio and television. He became news commentator in 1967, dealing mainly with scientific and technological subjects. Mr. Nagaoka is senior advisor to the Nuclear Safety Committee, the Council for Science and Technology and the Science Council of the Ministry of Education.

Energy Coverage—Media Panic

PART ONE

Oil Coverage

ONE

Energy Economics and Media Misinformation

Alan Reynolds

Vice-President and Chief Economist, Polyconomics, Inc.

Energy is a difficult subject, requiring both technical information and a grasp of the tools of economics. It is not surprising that the media have spread a lot of misinformation on this subject, particularly when the issue first became acute in 1974.

I began writing about energy economics as an editor with *National Review* magazine from 1972 through 1975, and so I am sympathetic to the rapid learning process which faced journalists at that time. We all made mistakes then, but it is less excusable today, after so many years of trial and error.

Before getting into the shortcomings of energy reporting, it is only fair to consider the constraints that make perfection an unreasonable goal. First of all, the press is rushed. Even the largest newspapers have staffs of only three or four dozen reporters, with four or five people covering Washington. Deadlines are often very tight, though this is less true of news and business magazines. Secondly, members of the press rarely have much technical expertise. The clubby Washington press corps, in particular, is composed of generalists who must cover a wide variety of political issues. The politicians too are rushed and often lack specialized expertise, so the media and politicians continually misinform each other.

Finally, there is a subtle pressure put on the press to limit criticism of government policies, since this can cut off a reporter's access to vital sources. This pressure tends to divert the media's attention toward finding fault in the private sector, rather than in public policies.

3

Journalists soon learn that clashes between people make better stories than clashes between ideas. As a result, serious issues become personalized, conveying the impression that reality is a matter of opinion. Objectivity is twisted into "Jones says this but Smith says that"—leaving the reader to discover the truth through innuendo, suspicion, or bias.

The journalistic search for objectivity also leads to giving inordinate attention to seemingly disinterested parties—typically those without any obvious economic or political motives. The press has often been naive in this respect, subject to exploitation by any group that cloaked itself in the mantle of public interest. Government agencies under political pressure, and ideological groups like Energy Action have been quick to learn that anything labeled "study" is uncritically advertised by the media. Yet any information from an oil company official, regardless of how accurate, is invariably treated as inherently suspicious.

"Oil industry spokesmen contend that they need high profits," wrote *Time* on May 6, 1974, "but others emphatically do not." Such a passage could *never* read: "Oil industry critics contend that profits serve no useful purpose, but industry spokesmen emphatically disagree." Industry spokesmen can only "contend" that something is true, while disinterested observers must show that they know better by being emphatic, loud, and angry. This is a standard formula.

The *New York Times*, on August 7, 1976, published an op-ed piece by Denis Hayes, a typical "disinterested source" from the "disinterested" Worldwatch Institute. Hayes argued that "energy growth does not lead to more jobs," and that we could cut fuel use almost in half "with only cosmetic changes in our style of life." Well, it is true that replacing tractors with shovels can increase employment, as can replacing computers and word processors with pencils. These are not "cosmetic changes." Millions would starve. Denis Hayes is not a disinterested source, but a zealot for the antiindustrial revolution. In *Progressive* (April, 1970) he was more candid about "mapping a struggle" against "the vested interests of the giant corporations" and "the paid-off senility of Congress." "We demand," said Hayes, "a lower productivity and a wider distribution."

The media never tell us anything about groups they cite—Worldwatch, Energy Action, or a number of other groups ostensibly representing consumers, citizens, or the public interest.

A fellow from Energy Action, Thomas Girard, graced the pages of the *New York Times* on April 19, 1977. He told us that natural gas producers "are guaranteed 18 percent profits above all their costs."

The *Chicago Tribune* on December 19, 1978 quoted "a spokesman for the Illinois Public Action Council, an energy public interest group." What kind of group is that? This fellow said the President should "force the major oil companies, mandate them, to begin producing domestic oil at a reasonable price." Howling nonsense. If these types of groups are going to be described as speaking for the public, or treated with any credibility and respect, reporters ought to do more investigating and tell us why we should take them seriously.

> Confronted with a sudden complicated issue, the press must find an explanation to offer. The reporters seeking it will typically have little technical knowledge. The explanation needs to be simply grasped by the public. Preferably it will center on people rather than impersonal technology. And to find it, reporters will look toward someone they believe has disinterested motives.
>
> These specifications can be met only by a limited range of possible explanations, almost by definition simplistic ones. Thus the early stages of press coverage of a new technical question are likely to be dominated by the Initial Simplistic Explanation.[1]

The "Initial Simplistic Explanation" is gradually eroded by facts and arguments, but it is never explicitly withdrawn. Its influence lingers on in public attitudes—perceptions of good guys and bad guys,—long after the dubious source of these attitudes is forgotten.

* * *

A fundamental problem, of course, is economic illiteracy within the media.[2] There are really only two schools of thought in economics—the right wing and the wrong. I state that in the semi-serious sense that meaningful statements about economic issues must be supported by evidence and logic, and not just by credentials and authority. The idea that economics is just a matter of opinion is fundamentally subversive and undermines the whole concept of rational choice.

Too often, the economic journalist adopts the lazy method of gathering opinions from various media-appointed "experts" without bothering to uncover and evaluate the reasoning, if any, behind those opinions. Even worse, many journalists have fallen into the nasty habit of simply asserting that "most economists agree" about this or that—as though they had conducted some formal opinion poll, and as though such a procedure was the appropriate method for separating truth from nonsense. Compounding the problem, the experts selected are often former government officials who tend to minimize governmental blunders or use partisan standards of performance.

Television news is almost entirely a recounting of each day's murders, fires, scandals, and sports scores, and so it is simply irrelevant to anything of lasting importance. When television does try to report economic issues, it is invariably botches the story so badly that one probably ought to leave bad enough alone. Television clearly picks its stories from the front pages of the *New York Times*, so we need to get back to the source.

The relevant media for economic information are not the publications themselves, but a tiny handful of editorial writers and reporters on each publication. Complaints about "the media" in the abstract are useless unless we realize that we are talking about real people. I will, therefore, concentrate on the print media, where time and story length are less constrained than with television. I will also define economic journalism broadly to include general columnists, editors who assign or reject outside articles, reporters, and editorial writers.

The common distinction between news reporting, which has an obligation to be fair, and editorial opinion, which has a right to be silly, seems inherently vague and arbitrary. At the *New York Times*, for example, Soma Golden has used the business section to complain about the persecution of radical economists on campus; Michael Jensen has used the front pages of the paper to advance the hypothesis that our energy problems are due to corporate greed; and Ed Dale (now with the Office of Management and Budget) once used the paper's magazine section to tell us that the Social Security System is in fine shape. I do not object to any of this, but no paper should expect to be immune to criticism for anything it prints, including signed columns and unsigned editorials. Statistics must be accurate, and analysis, rare as it is, must make sense.

It is probably unrealistic to expect newspapers and news magazines to present all sides of every issue with judicial impartiality. Journalism attracts passionate, power-hungry people who want to shape opinions and influence events. If journalists could somehow pretend to be as unopinionated as some people would like, the news would be very dull indeed. It is, above all, an entertainment industry, and inconclusive articles are not entertaining.

When it comes to economic issues, the real problem is not that media people fail to present the case for market-oriented policies fairly and impartially, but that they are sometimes genuinely unaware that any nongovernmental alternatives exist. Economists who are critical of government policies are not treated unfairly, they are simply ignored. To suggest meaningful change is to be dismissed by the media as ideological or (paradoxically) "conservative".

Despite all their posturing as muckrakers, most journalists are extraordinarily uncritical regarding government economic policies. News in this field is defined as a collection of government numbers, policies, and opinions, and so reporters soon acquire an unwholesome dependence upon government officials. The journalist who helps to advance the objectives of politicians or bureaucrats is the journalist who gets the leaks, early stories and interviews. With little criticism of government economic policies there is, is usually expressed in terms of personalities (e.g., moralizations about good policies being corrupted by evil people), rather than in analyses of the faulty design of the policies themselves. Hence, the scandals in Medicaid, HUD, or food stamps are never considered evidence against the programs themselves.

In desperate moments, I sometimes imagine that economics will have done all it can when it has taught journalists that demand falls and supply rises with higher prices. Consider this remark from the *New York Times* (June 3, 1977): "If the price were any higher it would produce only higher-cost energy, not more energy." That is, the supply curve for energy kinks at exactly the controlled price and either goes straight up or, perhaps, turns horizontally. On the demand side, here is a typical *Newsweek* economic analysis (April 18, 1977): "One alternative to conservation would be to decontrol all fuel prices." That seems to mean either that people would use more energy at higher prices, or that conservation is best encouraged with lower prices.

Put the above remarks together, and you have a situation in which prices do not affect either supply or demand, and therefore the government must direct everything. We have studies by the CIA and the Workshop on Alternative Energy Strategies that say just that, and it is a basic rule of journalism not to question anything that might be called a "study." Besides, the *New York Times* (April 6, 1977) informed us that "no one proposes . . . eliminating all price controls on oil and gas," and even my friend Bill Buckley (April 26, 1977) claimed that an OPEC-monopolized price is not really a "market price." So, using uncontrolled prices to bring energy supplies and demands into balance is an idea that must not even exist.

Another former colleague of mine, George Will, has written in *Newsweek* (April 18, 1977) that since we will run out of oil sooner or later, we might as well run out sooner. "Less than half of the U.S. energy is used in the production of goods and services," notes Will. "Most of it is used in individuals' consumption." Will is suggesting either that production for production's sake is less wasteful than production for individuals' consumption, or that direct consumption of energy for home heating or transportation is more wasteful than indirect consumption of energy in the forms of plastic bags, synthetic fabrics, and aluminum beer cans. Even some conservative journalists appear to have few doubts about their abilities to set priorities for other folks, and few reservations about letting some government agency decide who shall produce what and for whom.[2]

* * *

The initial failure of the media was in not warning us of the consequences of combining price controls on domestic oil and gas with inflationary monetary policy and increasing dependence on Arab oil. The predictable effect was an oil and gas shortage that put this country over a barrel.

In the April 1974 issue of *Intellectual Digest*, the economist Pierre Rinfret wrote that "no economist I know of ever mentioned the energy situation." This was not quite true. On June 2, 1972, the *National Review*

Bulletin warned of "our increasing reliance on the volatile Arab nations for rapidly growing U.S. oil requirements," and advised that "the nation's power crisis has already begun and is certain to grow worse." (Modesty prevents naming the author.) On August 10, 1973, the same journal wrote that "Saudi Arabia . . . is probably going to halt expansion of oil output, and to propose to other Arab oil nations they do the same." On November 1, 1972, *Congressional Quarterly* reported that "with the recent oil shortages, the OPEC countries have been able to increase their prices." On February 12, 1973, *Newsweek* noted that "spot shortages of fuel" were "almost a daily event." On May 7, 1973, the *Washington Post* observed that price "controls at this point would be no cure-all. A number of genuine shortages have now appeared. Petroleum products are the leading example." These brief warnings, however, were rare exceptions. In most cases, there was no reporting at all of the simple fact that holding U.S. oil and gas prices down was stimulating demand, discouraging supply, and causing OPEC prices to rise—long before the Arab embargo.

When the embargo broke out, there was a scramble to discover a simple explanation that would personalize the villain and not offend the government. The villain became "Big Oil," which supposedly conspired to create a phony shortage, fabricated statistics, and withheld supplies in order to fatten the profits. The task was made easier because Senator Henry Jackson and the F.T.C. were already waging a battle against "vertical integration" in the oil industry—something that has nothing to do with monopoly and which led nowhere.

*   *   *

The reporting of oil company profits by the media has often combined ignorance with demagoguery. In early 1974, we had this flash from the *New York Times*: "The first quarter profit returns are coming in, and the results are staggering—a mirror image of the prices that consumers are paying . . . Occidental Petroleum, a relative pigmy, increased its first quarter earenings by 718 percent."[3] On May 6, *Time* concurred that Occidental's profits were "stunning." Both reports neglected to mention that Occidental earned almost no profit the year before (6 cents per share down from 36 cents in 1962), so the percentage increase was meaningless. As for the "mirror image" of what consumers were paying. Occidental has insignificant petroleum operations in this country (some wells in Beverly Hills), but instead sells coal and chemicals.

Profit stories continually reported rates of change in profits, rather than profits as a percentage of sales or equity. (I unkindly pointed out, at the time, that oil company profit margins or rates of return were smaller than those of the *New York Times, Washington Post*, and the television networks.) The stories usually attributed all profits to domestic oil products, though they were largely due to European operations, coal, chemical, and natural gas production, tanker imports, and the devaluation of the dollar. There was no understanding of one-time inventory profits. Inventories of oil bought before the price increase created a paper profit when marked-up to the higher OPEC price, but that revenue had to be used later to replace the inventories at the new, higher price. Adjusted for inflation, those "staggering" first quarter profits of the 23 leading petroleum companies fell from $2.7 billion in 1974 to less than $1.9 billion in 1978. Needless to say, this was not widely reported, but the subsequent 1979 increase was.

The politicians were not enlightened by the media coverage. In a report to constituents in May, 1974, former Senator Alan Cranston of California wrote that "Gulf Oil, for example, reported profits of 153 percent in the final quarter of last year. Yet it paid only 2 percent of its income in federal income taxes." The erroneous implication is that profits were 153 percent of sales, when the true figure is usually closer to 5 percent. At best, the 2 percent tax refers to the U.S. tax relative to worldwide income, as though foreign wells, refineries, and gas stations should pay both foreign and U.S. income tax. A couple of years ago, James Johnston of Standard Oil of Indiana carefully calculated that federal, state, and local taxes were 27 cents per gallon of gasoline in Chicago, and foreign taxes were another 22 cents. That kind of calculation is never fit to print.

"Does our government have an urgent duty," asked the *Washington Post*, "to correct this vast enrichment of the oil companies? You bet it has." Aside from misunderstanding the nature of those profits and their role in allocating resources toward solving shortages, the *Post* exemplifies the constant introduction of egalitarian ethics into economic issues. If the purpose of a price system were to avoid the enrichment of those who invested in satisfying consumer demands, then we might as well price everything at ten cents and let people line up until supplies are gone. It is often fashionable to simply define poverty as a virtue and production as a sin. An otherwise encouraging article entitled "The Great Oil Rush of the Eighties" in the *New York Times Magazine* (August 30, 1981) just had to end by saying "it is clear that the profits from deregulation have not been equitably distributed." This would not be at all clear to any professor of ethics or welfare economics.

*   *   *

The profit story had to be muddled in order to fit the preconceived "Initial Simplistic Explanation," which was, of course, monopoly and conspiracy. Its most conspicuous spokesman was Michael Jensen of the *New York Times*, whose incompetent reporting has since been rewarded with one of the most prominent spots on television.

The Federal Energy Office (FEO) had a problem from the start. Some integrated refiners had invested in U.S. oil, most of which was kept cheap by price controls. Other refiners were deeply dependent upon imported oil, and there was no way to tell foreigners what to charge. Price controls were ostensibly designed to make retail prices of gasoline and heating oil depend on the average cost of crude. As a result, those producing refined products from domestic crude would have to charge less than those who were buying from OPEC. The import-dependent refiner could not compete.

The FEO first decided to make those refiners with cheap domestic crude share it with their rivals who had the foresight not to drill in this country. Refiners without domestic crude could get some by running short of the costly imported stuff. Refiners with domestic crude would have to share more of it if they imported more (at two or three times the price they gave theirs away). Nobody had much reason to import oil, so refineries ran at low capacity. A scandal to be sure, but who got the blame?

In the February 22, 1974 issue of the *New York Times*, Michael Jensen finally took notice of what was going on. Within the conspiracy model, the events could not possibly be the result of a failure of federal policy. Instead, the *Times* headline read: "Big Oil Concerns Are Cutting Back Imports of Crude: Deliberate Scarcities Laid to Unhappiness Over U.S. Allocation Program." Jensen wrote that "Some of the nation's major oil companies are *deliberately* reducing their imports of crude oil because they are *unhappy* with the Government's allocation program for crude, according to Administration sources." (Emphasis added.) A refiner who had to give $5 oil to a competitor had to replace it for $13. Yes, that made them unhappy, but it also made no sense. Jensen never explained any of this. Echoing the *Times* was an Associated Press dispatch five days later. It suggested the government's allocation scheme would be changed because "Some of the major companies are *unhappy* with the allocation program and are *deliberately* reducing their imports, Administration sources said recently." (Emphasis added.)

On February 23, George Meany, head of the AFL-CIO, even proposed nationalizing the oil industry, specifically citing Jensen's misleading story. In fairness, the *Wall Street Journal* had explained it all with characteristic accuracy on February 13 and *Newsweek* had revealed the masochistic allocation system ("The Cure is Worse than the Disease") on February 18. But Jensen's later piece did irreparable damage, and was particularly inexcusable in view of the earlier reports. All he had to do was scan the press before jumping to confusions.

Anyone who knew anything about energy had to suffer through a seemingly endless set of Jensen stories. The *New York Times* appeared determined to beat the *National Enquirer* for sheer excitement. A random sample of Jensen's work:

> *April 12, 1974*: "Rising Prices Fail to Spur Increase in Oil Production." This article observed that "critics say ... domestic oil production has dropped almost 2 percent in the last nine weeks." It neglected to mention that it takes years to find and develop new oil fields, and that nine-week data move up

and down quite often. By the second quarter of 1974, exploratory well completions were 61 percent above the level of a year before.

July 29, 1974: "Major Concerns Reduce Output Despite Oil in Plenty." This article talked about a *single* week, worrying that refineries were then running at 93 percent (92 percent is the maximum sustainable rate) rather than at the 99 percent figure of the same week a year earlier. The author's own data showed crude stocks up 9 percent, gasoline stocks up 9 percent, and stocks of other refined products up 14 to 22 percent. Yet Jensen wrote that unnamed "industry critics" said "the companies are deliberately restraining production to avoid price wars." (More is less?) Occidental's profits were "startling" again, as were Phillips, Sun (both British), and Conoco (mostly coal).

February 3, 1974: "Attacks on Oil Industry Grow Fiercer." The "owner of a small grocery" theorized that the oil companies "used the Arabs as an excuse to raise prices." An "associate of Ralph Nader" said the public was overcharged (always). A "professor of music" thought electric bills were unfair. The oil workers' union thought oil company profits were too high. A woman with a "huge old 16-room house" in Massachusetts found it expensive to heat. (This was news?)

August 12, 1975: "Deregulation of Crude Oil to Drive Up Cost of Fuels." Another "Ralph Nader lobbyist" said decontrol will add $900 to the average family's annual fuel bills. "Independent studies" by government agencies also "forecast dire consequences" from free markets. The author of *Highway Robbery* said decontrol will destroy independents.

What sort of information is all of this? Who on earth cares about what "Mrs. Paula Newcomb of Sacramento" thinks about energy? Who needs to be told that Ralph Nader's Sancho Panza thinks *all* prices are too high? What use is the conclusion of some "study" if the logic and evidence are not explained?

Officials in government agencies soon discovered that they could gain attention and look important by simply announcing that they would "investigate" anything that could be made to sound like an oil company conspiracy. The following is a very incomplete sample from, of course, the *New York Times*:

- June 10, 1975: "Gas Price Rigging Alleged by F.T.C."
- June 22, 1976: "F.P.C. Cites Lag in Reporting Natural Gas Reserves"
- October 14, 1977: "U.S. Tries to Find Oil Overcharges"
- February 17, 1977: "U.S. to Investigate Lag in Gas Output in Gulf of Mexico: Interior Secretary Andrus Wants to See if Producers Have Been Holding Back."

In all of these cases, and many more, when the reports eventually did come out, misconduct was never found, and the findings were either ignored or buried on a back page.

The story alleging rigged gas prices, however, was only a political game. One bureau within the FTC put together a sloppy memo on the subject, but economists shot it full of holes. Representative John E. Moss leaked the erroneous memo and suppressed the other, though the FTC never ended up making the purported allegation. The true story appeared in the *Dallas Times Herald* on June 14, 1975, but the political trick played on the *New York Times* had served its purpose.

If consumers keep extra fuel in their heating oil tanks or gasoline tanks, that is prudent conservation. If government stores oil in the ground, that is a strategic reserve. But if oil refiners keep the slightest extra inventory or fail to pump all oil and gas at a rapid pace, that is called "hoarding" or "withholding". There were annual accusations of withholding oil or gas, right up to the gasoline lines of 1979. None of the accusations proved correct. Several separate official investigations concluded that the gasoline lines in 1979, as in 1974, were mainly due to the Energy Department's price controls and allocation schemes. Even the DOE itself came to that conclusion. This was not widely reported.[4]

* * *

There was never the slightest evidence of monopoly or collusion in the domestic energy business, so nothing much came out of the media's cooperation in the feeble attempts to build political careers out of a non-issue. A typical Associated Press story appeared on July 31, 1977 and featured Senator Edward Kennedy's picture, a quote from Ralph Nader, and a headline about "Barring Energy Megamonopolies." There were the usual factual distortions. "Oil companies now supply about one fifth of U.S. coal production," said the A.P., but many of these "oil companies" (Conoco, Ashland, and Occidental) are big in coal but relatively small oil producers. "Twenty of the almost 100 firms involved in the mining of or exploration for uranium are oil companies," said the A.P. Again, one of the largest companies in uranium production, Kerr-McGee, is hardly big in oil. In 1976, all seven major oil companies combined accounted for less than 11 percent of coal production and less than 27 percent of uranium production. The A.P. story also worried that too many of the shale oil patents went to oil companies, as if to suggest that research were somehow monopolized or that shale production should be conducted by drugstore chains.

When the attacks on vertical and horizontal integration failed against the facts, the last assault was to prevent oil company investment in non-energy fields. Apparently, an oil refiner should not invest in producing oil, coal, uranium, or anything else. This was great fun for politicians while it lasted. Even the *Wall Street Journal* on February 9, 1976, gave front-page advertising to the unsupported complaints of Senators Bayh, Kennedy, and Tunney and Representative Conte. But the main damage was that the monopoly allegations diverted attention from the real problems and their solutions.

Errors of omission have been as troublesome as what the media has chosen to report. For example, the entitlements program replaced the original scheme that unduly discouraged oil imports with one that actually subsidized imports at the expense of domestic producers. This was difficult to understand or explain, so it was largely ignored.[5] Until recently, the issue of holding back energy exploration on 823 million acres of federal land also got short shrift, except in the *Wall Street Journal's* editorial pages. Another vital story almost universally neglected is the possibly huge potential of natural gas and oil exploration in developing countries. There was not even much attention paid to the World Bank's optimistic report *Energy in the Developing Countries* or to the United Nations' even more optimistic review of that report (published in *Important for the Future*, September, 1980).

Despite belated recognition that the Natural Gas Policy Act of 1978 was a disaster, the media keep repeating the myth that it nonetheless speeded-up gas exploration. In the two years before the act, drilling of gas wells increased by 20 percent and 25 percent. This dropped to 15 percent in 1978, 12 percent in 1979, 7 percent in 1980, and there was a decline in early 1981. Meanwhile, accelerated oil decontrol hiked oil drilling by over 39 percent in 1980. Prices work, if we let them.

The reporting of the economics of the energy issue remains sophomoric. There has been almost no recognition (always excepting the *Wall Street Journal*) of the idea that the dollar price of oil might have something to do with the value of the dollar. In fact, the media usually has that backwards. And there has been universal acceptance of the erroneous idea that retail prices of natural gas and gasoline are determined by the *average* costs that pipelines and refiners pay for the raw material.

* * *

Among the untold stories, there was no media inquiry into the question of who benefits and who loses from various energy policies. The media have consistently exhibited a narrow view of "special interests," identifying them as a variety of political, ideological, and financial blocs. In the enthusiasm of the moment, it apparently never occurred to the press that people could get rich from synthetic fuel subsidies, or tax credits that help sell insulation, gasohol, or wood-burning stoves. (Perhaps it is acceptable to make profits from subsidies, but not from market prices.)

Subsidies for coal-based synthetic fuel would be great for Ashland, Conoco, Exxon, and Gulf. Subsidies for squeezing oil from tar sands would be welcomed by Exxon, Gulf, Citgo, Sun, and Shell. Subsidies for oil shale would benefit Tosco, Superior, Occidental, and Union. President Carter's plan was essentially to finance such high-cost white elephants by putting an excise tax on producers of domestic crude—largely the independent wildcatters. Those reporters who described it as an attack on "Big Oil" were mistaken about who would be paying the "windfall" tax and who would be getting the subsidies.

Similarly, the crude-poor oil refiners did not necessarily mind controls on the price they paid for some small independent's crude oil. Big natural gas companies were not necessarily unhappy about similar controls put on the wellhead price of gas. Oil producers who are not much involved in natural gas production do not necessarily mind seeing this source of competition kept scarce by price controls on gas; neither does OPEC. The idea that there is a monolithic "oil industry" with a common interest is simply a myth.

The media never looked into the possibility that government regulation might benefit some businesses at the expense of others, or at the expense of consumers and taxpayers. Yet every government regulation benefits somebody, and the costly lobbying for regulations is rarely conducted by consumers. Keeping natural gas scarce and cheap may benefit those who are already hooked up (about half of all homes), but it certainly does not help those who are forced to use heating oil, propane, or electricity because of the artificial shortage.

Corporate ads should have given ample clues about who benefits from the manipulation of energy policy, prices, and subsidies. American Electric Power ran a full-page ad in the *Wall Street Journal* on February 4, 1976. It said "U.S. Proven Energy Reserves (They'll last about this long) Oil: 12 years; gas: 12 years; coal: 500 years." This was an outright lie, since reserves must be far more rigorously proven for oil and gas than for coal, and proven reserves are irrelevant anyway. Should we suspect that this advertiser produces coal?

The Southern Company had an ad in the *New York Times* on March 23, 1976: "Electricity can be generated from a variety of sources. And that's simply more efficient than using up our scarce resources." All supplies of electric power depend on burning scarce resources, and the transmission of electric power is generally far less efficient than burning the same fuels at the home or in a factory.

The nation's self-described "leading independent refiners" reprinted a column by Joseph Kraft, which at least should have made Kraft suspect something (*Wall Street Journal*, September 4, 1975). These "independents" were getting huge subsidies through the DOE entitlements program, and so they argued that "competition" cannot survive without price controls and subsidies.

Union Carbide ran an ad in the *New York Times* on October 29, 1979. It supported "financial incentives to speed the nation's investment in energy conservation projects." Should one suspect that this company either manufactures conservation materials or wants to buy some?

There is an untold story here, even now.

The uncritical acceptance of "studies" was nowhere more obvious than in the feature space devoted to anybody who would say we were running out of oil and gas, and that the only solution was massive conservation and subsidized solar power, synfuels, and gasohol:

- "Study Forecasts Major Shortages: Scientists Report the World Faces Future of Dwindling Oil and Mineral Supplies." *New York Times* (January 4, 1975).
- "U.S. Agency Sharply Reduces Estimate of Undiscovered Oil and Gas Reserves." *Wall Street Journal* (May 18, 1975).
- "Library of Congress Study Projects Mideast, North African oil to total 50% of imports in 2 years." *Oil and Gas Journal* (January 5, 1976).
- "World Oil Shortage Held Inevitable; Study Urges Move to Other Fuels" *New York Times* (May 17, 1977).
- "World Oil Output Could Decline 20% by 2000 Says Study" *Wall Street Journal* (October 20, 1980).
- "CIA Energy Study Issues Grim Forecast: Demand Will Far Exceed Supply by 1985." *Wall Street Journal* (April 20, 1977).

The second item on the list above deserved a follow-up in 1980, when the same agency, the U.S. Geological Survey, greatly *increased* its estimate of undiscovered oil and gas reserves (up 22% for gas). That wasn't news.

The other studies above are also already obsolete, vastly overestimating energy consumption and underestimating non-OPEC production. But the media do not keep track of past errors—they only report new ones, often from the same sources. These sorts of doomsday forecasts have been made every few years since 1920 for oil and since 1550 for firewood, whale oil, and coal. They are not getting any better with practice.

There are plenty of optimistic studies, too, but you will not find them in the mass media. "Oil Supply Crunch May Be Far Off New Study Asserts" appeared only in the expensive *Petroleum Intelligence Weekly* (November 3, 1980).

Exercises in arithmetic—"studies"—are a poor substitute for economic reasoning and political judgment, as we learned from the prolonged debate before the passage of the 1978 Natural Gas Policy Act (NGPA). The Carter administration then estimated a $70 billion cost to consumers by *assuming* that, with decontrol, prices above $1.75 per thousand cubic feed (mcf) would have no effect at all on supply, and that existing controls would somehow keep even unregulated intrastate gas at $0.70 in 1985 (it was already above $1.30 in 1977). Representative John Dingell's energy sub-committee *assumed* that uncontrolled gas would immediately soar to $5 per mcf—well above the then-prevailing cost of residual or heating oil—and that added supplies would not arrive until 1985 (when the study conveniently ended). Alice Rivlin's Congressional Budget Office ignored all "unconventional" sources of gas (at least 80 percent of U.S. resources) and *assumed* there would be a lot more drilling under the Carter plan.[6]

Rival studies by the deregulators (Representatives David Stockman and Bud Brown, and the Natural Gas Supply Committee) were able to come up with entirely different predictions by changing all these arbitrary assumptions. But it was a mistake for them to take the defensive, accepting the terms of the debate and the inherent limitations of econometric techniques. If the right questions are not asked, the right answers are unlikely to emerge. One question that was never asked was why we should *assume* that price controls on domestic raw materials should be effective in holding down final prices to consumers. In fact, there is ample evidence to the contrary.

*   *   *

Some technical errors are chronic, even to this day. The belief that "proved reserves" are a measure of what is available is one of the most persistent errors—probably because it supports a preconceived intellectual bias favoring enforced austerity ("conservation"). The idea is that we must save each ounce of oil, even if it requires a ton of aluminum or fiberglass to do so.

The *Reader's Digest* (August 1975 and November 1976) twice published James Nathan Miller's ridiculous claim that if only the natural gas industry did not make its own estimates of proved reserves, then there would somehow be plenty of gas available for all who wanted it at the controlled price. This sort of basic misunderstanding of the nature of "proved reserves"—which are just estimates of what is economically recoverable from presently known wells with existing technology and prices—even found its way into President Carter's first major energy address. Nobody in the media managed to spot it, although *Newsweek* later came close. Carter said that if world oil consumption continued to rise at a 5 percent rate, "we could use up all the proven reserves of oil in the entire world by the end of the next decade." Journalists were satisfied when told in a press conference that the much-publicized seven-page CIA study was the source of that dramatic remark. It is interesting that the CIA has suddenly become a respectable, unbiased source, but the CIA study actually said nothing about running out of reserves. It was a bad study, but it was not *that* bad. Global proved reserves of oil are now about two and a half times what they were two decades ago, which is a funny way to run out. According to *Petroleum Economist* (August 1980), worldwide *known* reserves of natural gas doubled over the past decade. Again, this was not worth reporting.

*   *   *

Another common technical error is the assumption that private automobiles are the main users of energy. This reflects the Eastern elite's chic contempt for any automobile (especially American) that can accommodate three children and the family dog. Those who get in and around

Manhattan or Washington D.C. by subsidized train cannot understand why others refuse to do the same in Texas or Kansas.

As it happens, private passenger cars only use about 15 percent of all energy and less than a third of the petroleum. Until the recent decline of oil imports, the United States would have been importing oil even if there were no cars at all. Did the American people get the mistaken impression from all the stories about "gas guzzlers" and our "love affair with the automobile"? Were we ever told that the costly efforts to make us buy smaller cars only brought the average miles-per-gallon to 14.3 in 1979—the same as in 1963?

* * *

Energy reporting has improved since 1974-76, but there are still some major lapses into long-discredited fallacies. One of the worst was by Donald Bartlett and James Steele entitled "Oil Prices: Is Villain OPEC, or Nearer Home?" (*Chicago Tribune*, August 5, 1979). This contained pure innuendo with no shred of logic or evidence.

Increases in oil profits are still front-page news and something to be "defended." But when the widely-predicted gains from decontrol failed to show up, the media were silent. "Big Oil's Profits Are Defended" appeared in the *Chicago Tribune* on July 29, 1979. Percentage increases were again described as "whopping" and we heard from the disinterested Citizen/ Labor Energy Coalition, but it was more balanced than its 1974 counterparts.

After all of these years of blatantly unfounded allegations by the Federal Tirade Commission, Washington officials can still get publicity with more of the same:

> "Oil Firm Probes Tied to Shortages Set by 2 Agencies: Justice's Antitrust Division, FTC Staff Seeking Cause of Low Gasoline Supplies." *Wall Street Journal*, May 16, 1979.

> "F.T.C. Aide Accuses Oil Companies: Lack of Gasoline Stockpiling Tied: A.P.-*New York Times*, June 12, 1979.

We remember those accusations, and perhaps forget that Alfred Dougherty's Bureau of Competition also instigated those earlier assaults that proved incorrect if not foolish. This time there were several such investigations. The result? "Reports Clear Oil Firms in Shortage" (*Chicago Sun Times*, July 17, 1980). The results are always harder to find and harder to remember than the original accusations. We are left with only a vague feeling that the government has been protecting us from the oil companies, when the opposite is probably closer to the truth.

The media still appear vulnerable to exploitation by special interest "studies." Even *Washington Report* (August 24, 1981), published by the

Chamber of Commerce, fell into a trap set by the natural gas pipeline companies. The report said decontrol must face "the political cost of probably doubling home heating bills just before the 1982 Congressional elections." The unnamed source of that "doubling" estimate is the American Gas Association, which *Time* (March 23, 1981) also naively cited as claiming that decontrol at the wellhead would "send up gas prices to the consumer by about 100 percent by 1982."

What decontrol would really do is raise average costs to the pipeline and distribution companies who have been fattening their gross profit margins by 9 percent a year, adjusted for inflation. Controls at the wellhead have *never* been able to hold retail gas prices to half the price of equivalent oil substitutes, and so the price could not possibly double.[7] Total energy prices to all consumers, including oil and electricity prices, would soon go down with decontrol—not up. There would be more domestic fuel, more competition for OPEC.

Economic analysis remains a weak link. In June and July of 1981, there was a series of articles suggesting the "oil glut" was almost over. The reasoning was dubious. *The Economist* (June 13, 1981) said "The Saudis are still pondering a 2 mbd (millions of barrels per day) reduction in their supply (as well as a $2 increase in their price)." Not likely. A little basic arithmetic shows that this would cost the Saudis $47.4 million per day. All the stories about the Saudis wanting to stabilize OPEC prices, or lower the prices in Nigeria, were Saudi propaganda. The Saudis simply wanted to grab a big share of the shrinking OPEC market by undercutting the cartel price.

In "Experts Say Oil Glut May Be Ending" (*Wall Street Journal*, July 16, 1981), John Lichtblau is quoted as having said "The amount of oil produced in the world today . . . isn't enough to meet world oil demand." (He said the opposite a month before in *The Economist*.) Yet the amount of oil purchased cannot exceed the amount sold, and volume alone cannot explain price. At the time, Iran and Nigeria were not producing much because their oil was overpriced, therefore the amount of world oil production looked small.

In "Downturn in Oil Prices May Not Last Long" (*Wall Street Journal*, July 8, 1981), Robert Pindyck said "with stable prices . . . an important source of demand reductions will gradually disappear." That is, prices will supposedly go up because people will not conserve so much if prices do not go up. (Pindyck is an economist, not a logician.)

*   *   *

Some rare but excellent media work deserves credit for the progress to date in discrediting the "Initial Simplistic Explanation." The best examples are the editorial page of the *Wall Street Journal*, Stephen Chapman's consistently informative pieces in the liberal *New Republic* (and now in the *Chicago Tribune*), scholarly essays in *The Public Interest*, and some of the in-depth reports in *National Journal*. Only one of these publications has a large circulation, but the power of good ideas has a tendency to spread and drive out the bad.

A few more awards are listed, necessarily incompletely, for excellent reporting and analysis of energy issues:

- *Forbes*: April 15, 1976: "Don't Blame the Oil Companies: Blame the State Department." How the U.S. created OPEC.
- "Gas Prices and Jellybeans," a *Washington Post* editorial by John Anderson, April 13, 1975. Holding natural gas prices down is like controlling the price of red jellybeans while black jellybeans (foreign oil) are free to reflect inflation. It makes red jellybeans scarce.
- "The Problem of Exhaustible Resources" by Stephen F. Williams, *National Review*, November 25, 1977. How markets adapt to and solve resource scarcity. Definitive.
- "Birth of a Superagency" by Michael Ruby et al., *Newsweek*, July 11, 1977. The Energy Department cost more than all the oil from Saudi Arabia, or all the profits of the seven largest oil companies.
- "U.S. Appears to Bear Oil-Shortage Brunt" by Steven Rattner, *New York Times*, May 29, 1979. Other countries did not have price controls and allocation schemes.
- "How to Think About Oil Profits" by Carol J. Loomis, *Fortune*, April, 1974. An early effort to put percentages in perspective. Not read by Michael Jensen.
- "How Little Oil Hit a Gusher on Capitol Hill" by Tom Alexander in *Fortune*, August 17, 1978. Joe Califano's achievement in getting huge entitlement subsidies for inefficient, teakettle refineries.
- "Renewable Energy: Asking Too Much of the Sun?" and "The Light Horse," *The Economist*, September 2, 1978 and September 27, 1980. Rigorous skepticism about fashionable but impossibly costly alternatives to oil and gas.
- "The Big Villain in Gas Crunch? Try Washington" by Ken Sheets, *U.S. News and World Report*, July 2, 1979. Pinning the tail on the right donkey.
- "Banana Oil: Government is to Blame for Shortages of Unleaded Gas" by Robert Bleiberg, *Barron's*, September 11, 1978. Different problems like banning M.M.T., but the same villain.
- "The New Gas Bonanza" by Merrill Sheils et al., *Newsweek*, October 30, 1978. There's a *lot* of natural gas at home if we'd allow it to compete with OPEC oil.

Reporters do learn, and those that do not generally find it harder and harder to get into print because their editors have learned. The most obvious errors of the 1974–77 period have been exposed, and the continual failure to substantiate the conspiracy theory makes new efforts in that direction look increasingly obsolete. Chronic failure of doomsday "studies" raises doubts about more of the same.

Experience with decontrolled oil—namely, a stronger dollar and the undermining of OPEC—has been too pleasant to support the implausible horror stories about decontrolling natural gas. Experience with gasoline waiting lines has been too horrible to support innocent enthusiasm for such primitive non-price methods of allocation in the future. Reality has reminded us that the price system, when left alone, is the best possible technique for moving resources toward uses that consumers prefer.

Summary

1. Many of the early media errors on energy can plausibly be excused by the hectic schedule of journalism, the lack of technical expertise, and the journalist's training to simplify and personalize stories. These forces led to the "Initial Simplistic Explanation"—namely, the allegation of collusion and conspiracy among major oil companies. All such charges have since been disproven but never withdrawn, so a vague suspicion remains implanted in the public consciousness.
2. The media's innocent search for "disinterested" sources has often led to its exploitation by groups that label themselves representatives of "the public interest." Also, anything described as a "study" is frequently reported without the slightest questioning of methods or evidence.
3. Reporters have failed to grasp the many ways in which government policies can be used to enrich seemingly noble causes, from natural gas pipeline companies to producers of gasohol.
4. Media dependence on Washington sources reinforces an apparent inclination to blame policy failures on private producers. Experts cited are often those with current or past experience in government, which compounds the problem. Government agencies gain publicity by announcing any "investigation" that often blames their own blunders on the victims.
5. Economic illiteracy is particularly hard to overcome, as indicated by the muddled moralizing about prices and profits. There has been little understanding that the only alternatives to rationing by price are to let government officials decide who gets what or to use the queue.
6. Technical errors persist, as evidenced by confusion about proved reserves, exaggeration of the potential of unconventional energy sources, and implicit exaggeration of the possible energy savings from smaller automobiles.
7. The futile search for a U.S. energy monopoly distracted attention from real issues. Among the errors of omission were an explanation of the entitlements subsidy for importing oil; the energy potential of developing countries or U.S. government land; the relationship of the value of the dollar to the dollar price of oil; fatal flaws in the Natural Gas Policy Act of 1978, and the subsequent slowdown in gas drilling; and any investiga-

tion of who would benefit from regulations or synthetic fuel subsidies, and who would pay.

8. Repeated doomsday stories about running out of oil and gas were unbalanced and have already been proven wildly inaccurate.

The quality of media coverage of energy is improving—largely because experience has discredited the early speculations and errors, but also because of a few pioneering efforts to really understand and explain key issues.

Notes

1. Jude Wanniski and Robert L. Bartley, "The Limits of the Press Corps in a Political/Technical Debate." Presented at a University of Chicago conference April 4-6, 1974.
2. This section is adapted from my 1977 talk to the Denver Economics Association, reprinted in *Studies in Economic Analysis* (University of South Carolina, Spring 1978).
3. The material on profits is from my article in the *National Review Bulletin* (May, 1974), reprinted in an anthology that I put together for *Conservative Digest*: "How the Liberals Are Causing the Energy Crisis" (1975).
4. For a detailed history of energy policy bungling, see my "A Free Market in Energy" in *Instead of Regulation*, ed. Robert Poole (Lexington, 1981). Also, Jack Kemp, *An American Renaissance* (Harper & Row, 1979) Ch. 7; and Joseph Kalt, *The Economics and Politics of Oil Price Regulation* (M.I.T. Press 1981).
5. An exception was my own "Why Subsidize the Arabs?" in *National Review* (August 29, 1975); also my "Slippery Oil: Energy Policy and Prices," *Argus Research* (September 8, 1975).
6. Michael J. Malbin, "Congress, Policy Analysis and Natural Gas Deregulation" in R. A. Goldwin, *Bureaucrats, Policy Analysts, Statesmen: Who Leads?* (American Enterprise Institute, 1980).
7. The evidence is in my "Decontrolling Natural Gas," Polyconomics (August 31, 1981).

TWO

German Media and Oil Supply in 1978 and 1979

Dr. Hans Mathias Kepplinger

Professor of Communications, University of Mainz

For several decades, communication researchers have been interested in the impact of mass media on society, although this was analyzed very seldom. Instead of the society or some parts of it—the economic system, the political system, and so on—individuals were studied and, instead of long-term processes, short-term reactions were analyzed. These research strategies were based on two underlying assumptions: first, the impact of the media on society is the sum of the impact on isolated individuals; second, the impact of the media on a social process is the sum of the impact on isolated actions. There are some doubts about these two assumptions. They neglect the interrelations between individuals and institutions as well as the self-dynamics of social processes in which the reporting of mass media intervenes through supporting or suppressing information.

On the other hand, there is of course good reason not to analyze the impact of mass media on society: one cannot experiment with societies as one can with individual subjects. The reason is quite simple: one does not have two equivalent groups of societies in one of which the manipulation of the variable under investigation—reporting of the mass media—could be controlled for experimental proof of the effects of mass media. Methodological expectations have not only steered research activities in the direction mentioned, but have also prevented communications researchers from looking

22

for similar designs which do not have the methodological quality of a controlled experiment, yet allow some conclusions which go beyond speculations.

Such a design may be given by comparing two similar historical processes in which the mass media intervened or did not intervene respectively. The expression "similar" here refers to what actually happened and not to what people thought was happening and to what the consequence of their image of reality was. Differences in the course of the two processes may then be attributed with some degree of certainty to the different roles played by the mass media. Such similarities between two processes existed in the 1973–74 and 1978–79 oil crises as far as the Federal Republic of Germany was concerned. In both of these situations, there was a political crisis which resulted in a decrease of crude oil production and an increase of crude oil prices; whereas the actual supply of fuel to the Federal Republic of Germany, the presentation of the situation by the media, and the reaction of the population were quite different.

The oil crisis in 1973–74 was analyzed in a previous study. Its results can be summarized as follows:

1. On October 6, 1973, the Yom Kippur War between Egypt and Israel broke out. The Egyptian army crossed the Suez Canal and conquered parts of the peninsula of Sinai within a very short time. After Israeli troops had reached the Egyptian bank of the canal and started to surround Egyptian troops, the war was ended under the pressure of foreign countries, especially the United States.

2. Most of the Arab countries regarded the political activities of the United States and other western countries as an interference in internal affairs that had deprived Egypt of a victory over Israel. Partly as a reaction to the Yom Kippur War, and partly as a consequence of a long-term strategy of OPEC, they started a series of decisions that changed the world's economy.

3. There were four types of decisions made by the petroleum-exporting countries in the fall of 1973: nationalization of private companies, price increases, limitations on output, and cutback on delivery.

4. Despite the decisions mentioned, the Federal Republic of Germany imported considerably more oil in September, October, and November of 1973 than in the same months of the previous year.

5. The mass media, especially in October and November, maintained that the supply of crude oil products to the Federal Republic of Germany was in danger.

6. In November, the public showed deep concern over the supply situation in the Federal Republic of Germany. There are no data available for October.

7. The population of the Federal Republic of Germany bought considerably more crude oil products in October and November than in the same months of the previous year.

8. The reserves of crude oil products decreased because of the increased demand. Simultaneously, short-term delivery problems occurred.
9. The mass media labeled this development a "crisis," and named the petroleum-exporting countries and the multinational oil companies as the agents of this so-called "crisis."

It was argued that the speculation of the mass media on an "oil crisis" formed something like a "critical mass" which initiated a self-steering process: the false image of reality stimulated the demand for crude oil products. This resulted in a shortage of supply which seemed to confirm the expectations and in turn further stimulated the demand. Thus, even those who had not read the messages in the newspapers, or heard them on radio or television, were indirectly influenced by the media. The reporting by the mass media in that sense was the "condition *sine qua non*" of the so-called "oil crisis" of 1973–74, which never had to happen based on the actual supply situation (Kepplinger, Roth, 1978, 1978b).

The political situation in the Middle East in 1978–79 was overshadowed by the revolution in Iran. Since January 1978, a series of violent demonstrations against the authoritarian regime of Shah Mohammed Rezah Pahlevi shocked the political system. On August 27, Prime Minister Jamshild Amouzegar, who had been a major representative of the old regime and one of the leading figures of OPEC, resigned. He was followed by Jafar Sharif Emami who started a policy of liberalization in an attempt to calm down the revolutionary masses. To undermine the new policy, on September 7, Ayatollah Madari proclaimed a general strike which was widely followed all over Iran. In late September, although strikes had been declared illegal, about 10,000 workers in the oil industry went on strike. On October 31, a new general strike paralyzed Iran's oil export.

On November 6, one day after revolutionary riots in Teheran, Jafar Sharif Emami was replaced as Prime Minister by General Gholam Reza Azhari who sent troops to the oil fields, yet remained unable to start the oil production again. In late December, gasoline and diesel fuel were rationed, but the general strike went on. On December 31, General Gholam Reza Azhari resigned as Prime Minister. His successor was the leader of the National Front, Shapur Bakhtiar, who had been in opposition to the Shah for several years. Although Bakhtiar was nominated as Prime Minister by both Houses he was labeled a traitor by the revolutionary opposition in the streets. The economic situation remained critical, the strikes went on, and the internal and external support for the Shah trickled away. On January 16, 1979, Shah Mohammed Reza Pahlevi left Iran. His departure was followed by transports of joy in the streets of Teheran.

As conqueror over the Shah, Ayatollah Khomeini, who had been in exile for 15 years, returned to Iran on February 1, 1979. He proclaimed an Islamic Republic and made Mehdi Bazarghan Prime Minister of a provisional government. Some days later a revolt broke out among the troops and resulted in an alliance between the army and the provisional government. On February 11, Prime Minister Bakhtiar resigned and later left the country. In a plebiscite on April 1, 1979, about 99 percent of the population voted for the Islamic Republic but on a lower level the internal riots went on during the summer of 1979 (Archiv der Gegenwart 1978/1979).

Simultaneously with the developments in Iran, the Organization of the Petroleum Exporting Countries (OPEC) made some decisions with far-reaching consequences. On December 17, 1978, OPEC decided to increase the price for crude oil in four steps by 14.5 percent. The four steps would be made on January 1, April 1, July 1, and October 1, 1979. However, as a reaction to the decrease of the oil production in Iran and to the increase of the oil price in Rotterdam, on March 26-27, 1979, OPEC decided to make the price increase at once in one step. On May 26-27, OPEC again increased the oil price, this time by 23.7 percent, which resulted in a total increase of 41.7 percent since January 1979.

During the whole process, the oil exporting countries and the multinational oil companies accused each other of artificially increasing the oil price and each legitimated its own decisions by those made by the other side. The oil exporting countries argued that they would not leave the total profit to the multinational companies, while the multinational oil companies argued that they had to raise the price because the oil exporting countries had done so first. Thus, the revolution in Iran resulted in the most profitable business years for the oil exporting countries and the multinational oil companies—and brought on the most serious economic crisis of the western industrial societies since World War II (Archiv der Gegenwart 1978/1979).

Because the crisis in Iran as well as the decisions made by OPEC culminated at the turn of 1978-79, it was decided to analyze the half-year period before and the half-year period after that date. Thus, the analysis starts with July 1978 and ends with June 1979. This gives us the chance to detect the very beginning of the crisis and the direct consequences of the major events and decisions.

The oil production of Iran sank, according to the National Iranian Oil Company (NIOC), from 5.4 to 5.5 million barrels per day before the political crisis to 1.15 barrels per day on November 7, 1978. In January 1979, the production was even lower. It was not until March 1979 that the oil production increased to 2.5 million barrels per day, but even in August 1979, with 4 million barrels per day, it had not yet reached the level of the previous years.

Despite the fact that the decrease in oil production had already begun in 1978, Iran in 1979 produced about 109.5 million tons less oil than in 1972. Figure 2.1 shows the decrease in the oil production in Iran from 1978 to 1979 which was compensated by an increase of the oil production elsewhere, especially in Saudi Arabia, Iraq and Nigeria. Therefore, comparing the full years, there were no remarkable decreases in oil production in 1979 as compared with 1978.

FIGURE 2.1   Production of Crude Oil 1979 in Comparison to 1978

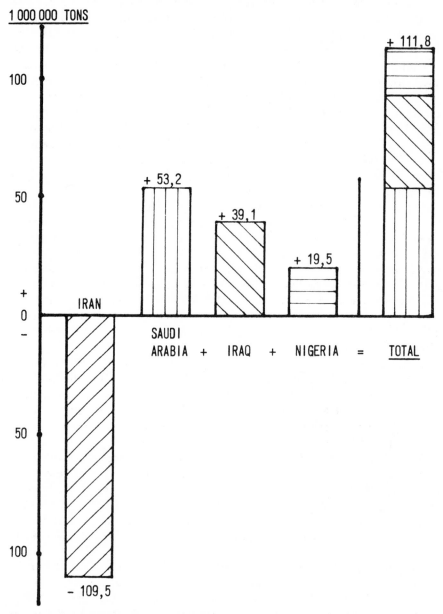

Source: *Petroleum Economist*, June 79/May 80

The overall comparison of oil production in 1978-79 does not give an adequate picture of the supply situation during the Iranian crisis. Actually, the breakdown of oil production in Iran after October 1978 was followed by a remarkable decrease in the total world oil production in January and February of 1979. As a consequence, in these two months, there was a severe shortage in crude oil which would have had a disastrous impact on world economics if it had lasted. Figure 2.2 shows total world oil production and oil production in Iran in 1978 and 1979. A more detailed analysis of world crude oil production in 1978-79 shows why the breakdown of oil production in Iran in October, November, and December of 1978 did not at once result in a reduction in total world production. During that time, Saudi Arabia had increased its production to maximum level. On the other hand, the actual shortage in January and February of 1979 was the result of a remarkable decrease in oil production in Saudi Arabia. Thus, it was the decision of Saudi Arabia not to compensate for the total deficit which caused the shortage in January and February of 1979. On the reasons for that decision one can only speculate. It would not be totally wrong to assume that Saudi Arabia intended to underline the decision of OPEC of December 17. A shortage of oil could help to force through an increase in the oil price. Figure 2.3 shows the oil production of the most important suppliers to the Federal Republic of Germany in 1978-79.

In 1978/1979 Iran was one of the most important suppliers of oil to the Federal Republic of Germany. Despite that fact, the breakdown of the oil production in Iran did not at once influence the supply to Germany, because the deficit was compensated by other countries. Actually, Germany was not dependent on Iran, but on the international oil market. When the total world oil production decreased in January and February of 1979, there was a sharp decrease in oil imports into the Federal Republic of Germany. Therefore, in contrast to 1973-74, 1979 presented more serious problems of supply to the Federal Republic of Germany.

Figure 2.4 shows the total world production, the production of Iran, and the importation of oil into the Federal Republic of Germany. A more detailed analysis of the supply situation to the Federal Republic of Germany shows how it was possible to overcome the serious situation in spring 1979. When the breakdown of oil production in Iran began, the shortage was at first compensated by Saudi Arabia, Algeria, and the United Kingdom, which exported more oil to the Federal Republic of Germany than before. They were followed by Libya and Nigeria. When the shortage was most serious, in February and March of 1979, Saudi Arabia, Algeria, Nigeria, and the Arab Emirates increased their oil exportation to Germany. Figure 2.5 shows the decrease and increase in oil importations into the Federal Republic of Germany in 1978 and 1979.

The price of oil, when crossing the border of the Federal Republic of Germany, was influenced only slightly by the crisis in Iran. There was, of

28

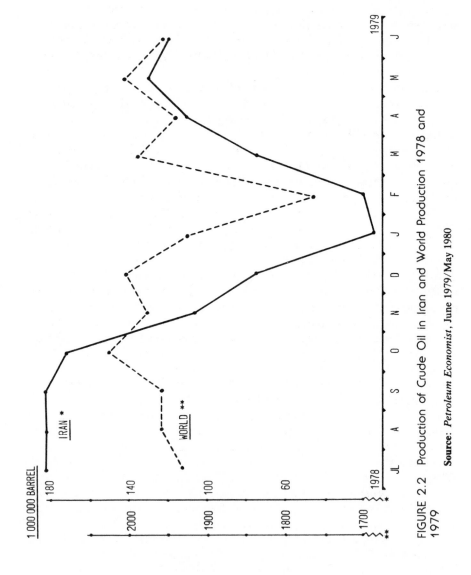

FIGURE 2.2 Production of Crude Oil in Iran and World Production 1978 and
1979

Source: *Petroleum Economist*, June 1979/May 1980

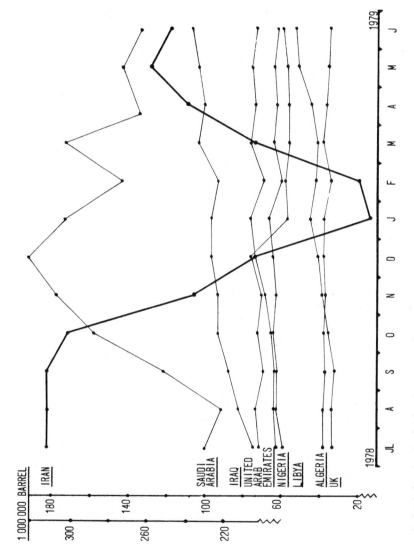

FIGURE 2.3   Crude Oil Production of the Most Important Suppliers to the F.R.G.
Source: *Petroleum Economist*, June 1979/May 1980

29

30

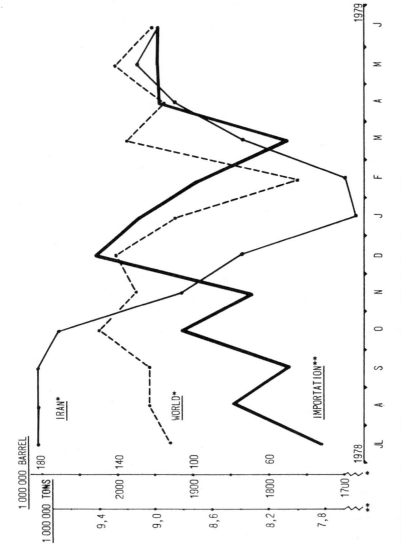

FIGURE 2.4   Crude Oil Importation into the F.R.G. (For Purpose of Comparison:
World Production, Production of Iran

Source: *Bundesamt Für Gewerbliche Wirtschaft* 79/80; *Petroleum Economist,*
June 79/May 80

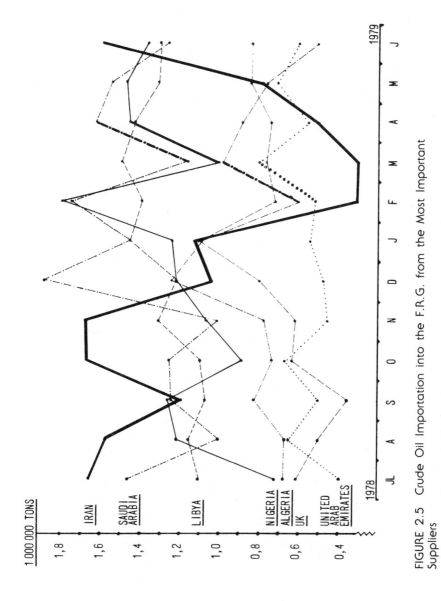

FIGURE 2.5   Crude Oil Importation into the F.R.G. from the Most Important
Suppliers

Source: *Bundesamt für Gewerbl. Wirtschaft Mineralölstatistik 1979/1980*

31

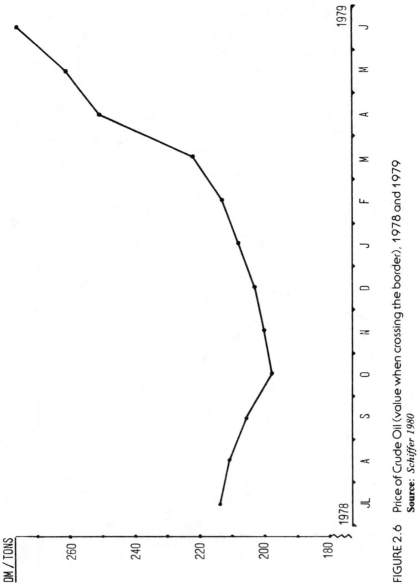

FIGURE 2.6   Price of Crude Oil (value when crossing the border), 1978 and 1979
Source: *Schiffer 1980*

32

course, since October, when the breakdown of the oil production in Iran began, a steady but slight increase in the oil price. But it was not until March that the dramatic increase began which shocked the German economy. At that time, oil production in Iran was already increasing. Therefore, there is good reason to assume that it was neither the political crisis in Iran nor the shortage of supply which caused the development. It seems that these events were used partially to legitimate the decisions made by OPEC and some multinational oil companies. They actually seem to have caused the dramatic increase in the oil price in the spring and summer of 1979. Figure 2.6 shows the development of the price of oil when crossing the German border in 1978 and 1979.

Summarizing the situation of the Federal Republic of Germany in 1978 and 1979, one can draw two main conclusions. First, despite a slight increase in the winter of 1978 – 79, there was at that time no serious problem with the oil price. Second, this problem really did not begin until just before March of 1979, and it increased dramatically in the summer of that year.

The supply situation was quite different. Whereas the crisis in Iran in 1978 did not influence the German situation, in February and March of 1979, there was a serious shortage of oil in the Federal Republic of Germany as a result of the decrease in the world oil production. This dangerous situation was overcome mainly by increased importations from some Arab countries.

Three national quality newspapers, *Süddeutsche Zeitung, Frankfurter Allgemeine Zeitung* and *Die Welt*, were chosen for a quantitative analysis of the reporting of the oil crises in the mass media. The three newspapers represent different political views, from liberal to conservative. Taken together, they give a fairly good picture of the distribution of various political views in the German mass media. An investigation covered the period from July 1, 1978 to June 30, 1979. The first four pages of every second edition were analyzed, as well as the first four pages of the economic section of each newspaper.

All articles were covered which had in their headline one of the following catchwords: *Iran, OPEC, oil, gasoline, energy,* and *crisis*. A total of 1,331 articles were analyzed. The *Süddeutsche Zeitung* published 422 articles, the *Frankfurter Allgemeine Zeitung* published 420 articles; and *Die Welt* published 471 articles. In 626 articles Iran was mentioned and among these were 354 articles on political problems only and 272 articles ·on oil as well. Thus, during the twelve months under investigation the three newspapers published a total of 977 articles on oil.

In 1973 – 74, the same three newspapers had published a total of 1,244 articles during a six-month period. The two figures indicate that the first oil crisis was much more a media event than the second one. This conclusion may be underlined by the fact that during the first six-month period the newspapers mentioned the word *crisis* in more than 600 articles, whereas during the second twelve-month period they mentioned it in only 145 articles.

The three newspapers published 2,112 statements on oil production (supply), oil consumption (demand), and oil prices. Taking statements on the Federal Republic of Germany and other countries together, most attention was given to supply (1,005 statements), followed by the development of prices (909 statements), and consumption (198 statements).

As to statements concerning the Federal Republic of Germany only, most attention was given to the development of prices (519 statements), followed by supply (312 statements), and consumption (117 statements). These figures indicate that supply was seen at first as an international problem, which for Germany ranked only second in importance. The most serious problem for Germany seemed to be the development of the oil price.

This impression can be strengthened by comparing positive and negative statements. "Positive" here refers to all statements saying that the situation was good (normal) or would become better; "negative" here refers to all statements saying that the situation was bad (abnormal) or would become worse. In respect to the supply of oil, 42 percent of all statements were positive, and 58 percent were negative. Regarding the consumption of oil, the figures were similar with 40 percent positive and 60 percent negative. Quite different was the reporting on the oil price. Only 13 percent of all statements were positive, whereas 87 percent were negative.

From these figures one can draw the conclusion that the three newspapers presented the situation to their readers mainly as a crisis of the oil price. If one looks on the period under investigation, this impression was partly wrong; but if one looks on toward future development, it was quite right.

Most statements concerning the supply of oil dealt with the production of crude oil and the supply of crude oil products. The proportion of negative statements among all statements was, as already mentioned, 58 percent. In respect to these aspects, the reporting on the supply of oil in 1978–79 was similar to the reporting in 1973–74. In contrast to the first period, in the second period the shortage was not seen as having been artificially made. There were few statements regarding delivery cutbacks by the petroleum-exporting countries, but there was no statement on artificial shortages by the oil companies. These figures indicate that in 1978–79 the shortages were not seen as consequences of a conspiracy, as they were to a certain degree in 1973–74. Thus, the role played by the petroleum-exporting countries and by the oil companies was perceived differently.

There is another difference in the reporting which underlines previous findings. In 1978–79, the proportion of statements expressing expectations (speculations) was lower than in 1973–74—37 percent to 43 percent.

TABLE 2.1 POSITIVE AND NEGATIVE STATEMENTS OF FACT AND EXPECTATION CONCERNING THE SUPPLY OF CRUDE OIL AND CRUDE OIL PRODUCTS TO THE FEDERAL REPUBLIC OF GERMANY, AS SEEN IN THREE NEWSPAPERS.

Subject of Statements	Statements of Fact			Statements of Expectation			All Statements			Foreign Countries	Foreign Countries and F.R.G.
	Pos.	Neg.	Total	Pos.	Neg.	Total	Pos.	Neg.	Total	Total	Total
The Energy Supply in General	1	2	3	2	6	8	3	8	11	11	22
Crude Oil Production for the F.R.G.	71	123	194	46	38	84	117	161	278	255	533
Supply of Crude Oil to the F.R.G.	15	27	42	15	15	30	30	42	72	76	148
Supply of Crude Oil Products to the F.R.G.	32	32	64	23	39	62	55	71	126	90	216
Crude Oil and Crude Oil Product Reserves	18	16	34	6	4	10	24	20	44	32	76
Artificial Shortages by the Oil Companies	0	0	0	0	0	0	0	0	0	—	0
Delivery Cutbacks, Boycott of F.R.G.	0	3	3	0	7	7	0	10	10	—	10
Total	137	203	340	92	109	201	229	312	541	464	1005

Note: Only those statements which pertained to the Federal Republic of Germany were taken into consideration. In the case of "delivery cutbacks," general statements were also taken into consideration, in so far as they did not pertain explicitly to other countries. "Positive" connotes that the supply situation is good or improving, "negative" connotes a bad or worsening supply situation. In the case of "delivery boycott," the term "positive" signifies that no boycott takes place, and "negative" that it does take place. The same pertains to the term "artificial shortages."

Regarding the proportion of speculations as an indicator of the seriousness of a crisis, one can conclude that the situation in 1973-74 was seen much more as a crisis than the situation in 1978-79. Table 2.1 shows details of the reporting on the supply of crude oil and crude oil production.

Most statements on prices dealt with the price of crude oil followed by statements on the price of crude oil products and the price of gasoline. Similar to the statements on supply, most statements were negative. In contrast to the statements on supply, more statements of fact than statements of expectations were published. From this one can conclude that the increases in prices were taken as a matter of fact, whereas shortages of supply were seen as possibilities only. This may have focused the attention of the public in Germany on price increases and as a result, the shortages were not given as much consideration. Table 2.2 shows details of the reporting on prices of crude oil and crude oil products.

Most statements on consumption dealt in a relatively global manner with the demand for crude oil products, followed by statements on the demand for gasoline. Similar to the reporting on the previous topics, most statements were negative. But in contrast to statements on supply and price, there were more positive than negative expectations. The difference is small, but as a deviant case it is remarkable. It seems to indicate that the newspapers did not expect the solution of the problem to be a decrease in prices or an increase in production, but rather a reduction in consumption in the country. These expectations, in fact, were to a certain degree fulfilled. Table 2.3 shows details of the reporting on the consumption of crude oil and crude oil products.

The picture already presented can be completed with some additional data. There were relatively few statements on the causes of the situation. Among all causes, the crisis in Iran (n = 62)* was mentioned most often, followed by the consumption of oil products in the United States. Statements on the consequences of the situation were relatively rare, too. Among all consequences, a global increase of consumer prices (n=27) and a reduction of trade (n=27) were mentioned most often.

In contrast to the reporting on these topics, there were many more statements on measures which should or could be taken. Most often, a reduction in national consumption (n = 84) was demanded, followed by demands for a new attitude towards energy consumption (n = 46), and an increased use of coal (n = 43) and nuclear energy (n = 43). Very seldom were price controls (n = 3), rationing (n = 4), prohibition on driving (n = 13), and other legislative measures (n = 17) demanded. These figures indicate that most commentators opposed governmental regulations and supported the market system.

Reporting on oil increased rather slowly in 1978-79, in contrast to 1973-74. From July to October of 1978 the total number of articles covered, the number of articles on oil, and the number of articles on Iran

* "n" stands for number of times mentioned.

TABLE 2.2 POSITIVE AND NEGATIVE STATEMENTS OF FACT AND EXPECTATION CONCERNING THE PRICES OF CRUDE OIL AND CRUDE OIL PRODUCTS TO THE FEDERAL REPUBLIC OF GERMANY, AS SEEN IN THREE NEWSPAPERS.

Subject of Statements	Statements of Fact			Statements of Expectation			All Statements			Foreign Countries	Foreign Countries and F.R.G.
	Pos.	Neg.	Total	Pos.	Neg.	Total	Pos.	Neg.	Total	Total	Total
Price of Crude oil	7	106	113	3	55	58	10	161	171	162	333
Price of Crude Oil Products	4	84	88	7	56	63	11	140	151	119	270
Price of Gasoline	14	64	78	7	23	30	21	87	108	77	185
Price of Light Fuel	11	47	58	11	11	22	22	58	80	29	109
Price of Heavy Fuel	1	7	8	0	1	1	1	8	9	3	12
Total	37	308	345	28	146	174	65	454	519	390	909

Note: Only those statements which pertained to the Federal Republic of Germany where taken into consideration. "Positive" connotes that the price remains stable or decreases, "negative" connotes that the price increases.

TABLE 2.3 POSITIVE AND NEGATIVE STATEMENTS OF FACT AND EXPECTATION CONCERNING THE CONSUMPTION OF CRUDE OIL AND CRUDE OIL PRODUCTS TO THE FEDERAL REPUBLIC OF GERMANY, AS SEEN IN THREE NEWSPAPERS.

Subject of Statements	Statements of Fact			Statements of Expectation			All Statements			Foreign Countries	Foreign Countries and F.R.G.
	Pos.	Neg.	Total	Pos.	Neg.	Total	Pos.	Neg.	Total	Total	Total
Demand of Crude Oil Products	0	2	2	1	1	2	1	3	4	6	10
Consumption of Crude Oil	3	4	7	4	5	9	7	9	16	13	29
Consumption of Crude Oil Products	9	19	28	12	7	19	21	26	47	39	86
Consumption of Gasoline	3	15	18	1	1	2	4	16	20	13	33
Consumption of Light Fuel	7	11	18	2	4	6	9	15	24	6	30
Consumption of Heavy Fuel	4	1	5	1	0	1	1	1	6	4	10
Total	26	52	78	21	18	39	47	70	117	81	198

Note: Only those statements which pertained to the Federal Republic of Germany were taken into consideration. "Positive" connotes that the consumption increases, "negative" connotes that the consumption remains stable or decreases.

(without mentioning oil) remained nearly the same. Thus, the political problems in Iran, including strikes in the oil business, had no remarkable impact on the press coverage in that period.

It was not until November 1978, when General Gholam Reza Azhari became Prime Minister and sent troops to the oil fields, that the number of articles on the topics mentioned increased. Until February 1979, reporting on political problems in Iran and on oil continued to increase, whereas the number of articles on political problems dropped. The decline in the number of articles on the political situation in Iran after the Shah had left the country and Khomeini had taken power indicates that the three newspapers viewed the political crisis as being over. This impression was possibly mistaken. Figure 2.7 shows the number of articles on different topics from July 1978 to June 1979.

Comparing the oil importation to the Federal Republic of Germany and the press coverage of the supply to Germany, one finds no clear correlation. Actually, in February and March of 1979 there was a sharp decline in oil importation to Germany. During these two months, the number of negative statements in the newspapers reached its maximum. From this, one could conclude that the press gave an adequate picture of reality. But in June, when the supply was quite good, the number of negative statements increased again. More than that, in February and March, when the supply was critical, the number of positive statements on supply reached its maximum. Therefore, one can conclude that the increases in both negative and positive statements on supply were caused partly by the increase in the number of articles published in February and March, and thus, they reflect not only insight into the situation but also the volume of publication.

In February 1979, when the supply became critical, the newspaper reader was given a negative but contradictory picture of reality. During that month, the three papers under investigation published 102 statements on the supply to the Federal Republic of Germany. The ratio of positive and negative statements was 41:61. This was quite different from the reporting in November of 1973 when the supply was much better than in March of 1979. In November, 1973, the three papers published 226 statements on the supply to the Federal Republic of Germany. The ratio of positive and negative statements was 57:169. Thus the press in 1973 gave a clear impression of a crisis situation.

If one takes into consideration the relatively small number of articles in February, 1979—compared to November, 1973, the relatively small number of statements on the supply to the Federal Republic of Germany, and the contradictory content of these statements, one can conclude that in 1978–79 there were no stimuli which could have formed something like a "critical mass." Figure 2.8 shows the number of positive and negative statements on the supply to the Federal Republic of Germany.

40

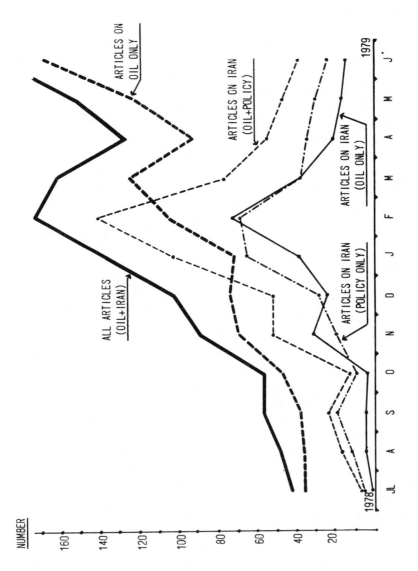

FIGURE 2.7   Number of Articles on Different Topics

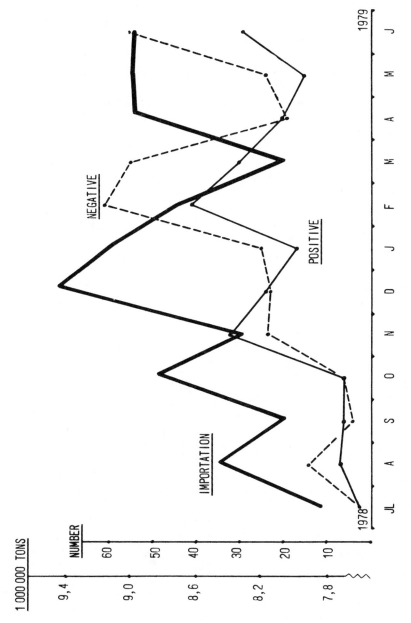

FIGURE 2.8 Positive and Negative Statements in the Press Concerning the Supply of Crude Oil and Crude Oil Products to the Federal Republic of Germany (for Purpose of Comparison: Actual Importation to F.R.G.)

41

Comparing the actual price of oil and the reporting of the three newspapers on the price of oil, there was, with the exception of January and April, 1979, a clear correlation: the increase in the oil price was accompanied by an increased number of negative statements on the oil price in the three newspapers. The two exceptional months are hard to explain, especially because they follow the decisions of OPEC in December, 1978 and in March, 1979. Maybe all relevant statements were already published in December of 1978 and March of 1979 or maybe the decisions were not taken very seriously before their consequences could actually be felt some weeks later—there is no clear explanation. Figure 2.9 shows the number of positive and negative statements on the price of oil.

Similar to the reporting on the supply of oil, the reporting on the consumption of oil products in the Federal Republic of Germany draws a contradictory picture. During most of the time, the numbers of positive and negative statements on the consumption were similar. The two exceptions are August, 1978 and June, 1979 during which the negative statements dominated. But there was no clear correlation between the negative tendency of the press coverage and the actual behavior. Figure 2.10 shows the number of positive and negative statements on the consumption of crude oil products.

In contrast to 1973–74, there was no panic reaction of the population in the Federal Republic of Germany in 1978–79. The reaction of the people was so calm that one of the big oil companies, which charged the Institut für Demoskopie Allensbach with performing regular surveys on the concerns of the population, did not ask a question on the supply of oil until July, 1979. Then, they used the same two-part question which they had asked every second week in the winter of 1973: "Do you believe that gasoline could become so short in supply in the next two or three months that serious supply situations will arise? Or do you believe that such fears are exaggerated?"

In the winter of 1973–74 about 70 percent of the population feared serious problems. In the summer this belief was held by 23 percent, and in the winter of 1979–80 by 19 percent only. These figures clearly indicate that there was no fear of an oil crisis in Germany in 1979 (Allensbacher Archiv, Institut für Demoskopie Allensbach).

As a result of the definition of the situation, the consumer behavior in 1978–79 was quite normal. The only exception was January of 1979 when consumers bought more light fuel and heavy fuel and less gasoline because of an extremely cold and snowy winter. The increase in demand for fuel and the decrease in demand for gasoline resulted in an overall increase in demand for all products.

In February, 1979, when the number of negative statements on the supply situation to the Federal Republic of Germany slightly increased, and in March, when the actual supply situation became critical, consumer behavior

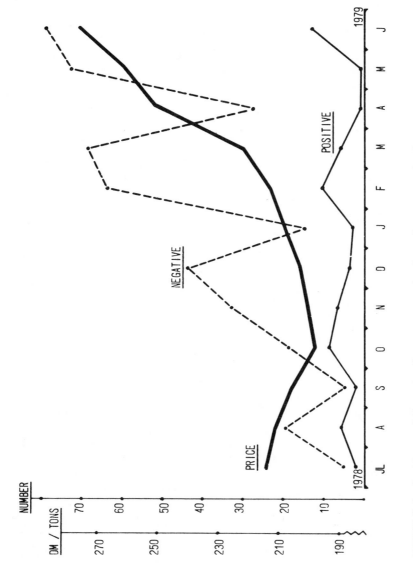

FIGURE 2.9 Positive and Negative Statements in the Press Concerning the Price of Crude Oil and Crude Oil Products in the F.R.G. (for Purpose of Comparison: Actual Price of Crude Oil)

43

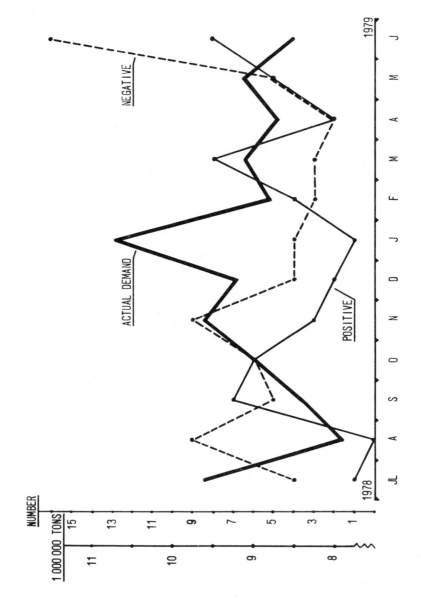

FIGURE 2.10 Positive and Negative Statements in the Press concerning the Demand for Crude Oil and Crude Oil Products in the F.R.G. (for Purpose of Comparison: Actual Demand—All Products)

44

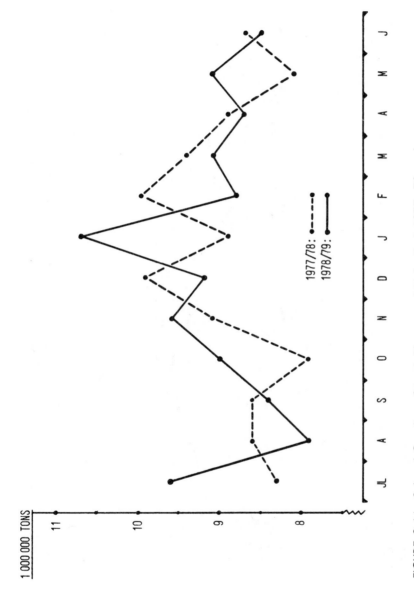

FIGURE 2.11 Sale of Gasoline, Diesel, Heavy and Light Fuel 1977–78 and
1978–79

Source: *Mineralölwirtschaftsverband* 1980

45

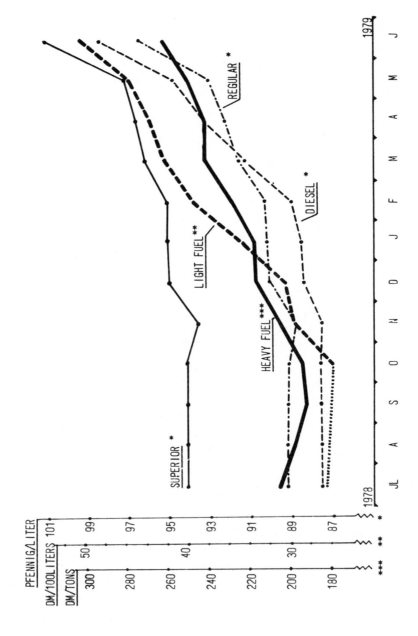

FIGURE 2.12   Price of Oil Products to Consumers in 1978 and 1979 (Incl. Tax)
Source: *Schiffer 1979/Schiffer 1980*

46

was already quite normal. Figure 2.11 shows the demand for crude oil products in the twelve-month period under investigation and in the previous twelve-month period.

The price for superior, regular, and gasoline in Germany increased slightly from December 1979 to March 1979. From then, the increase became bigger and bigger. On the market for light and heavy fuel, there was a bigger increase in prices already since November, 1978, and the development was more steady than on the market for superior, gasoline, and diesel. But on all these markets there were no sudden and dramatic changes as in 1973–74. There was, especially, no visible impact of the critical supply situation in February and March of 1979 on the prices of oil products. Figure 2.12 shows the prices for oil products in Germany in 1978 and 1979.

Summary and Conclusions

The analysis of the oil crisis in 1978–79 in the Federal Republic of Germany can be summarized as follows:

1. The revolution in Iran and the decision of Saudi Arabia to reduce its increased production had a remarkable impact on the supply of oil to the Federal Republic of Germany, especially in February and March of 1979. It created a serious shortage of importations.
2. The press did not treat the situation as a crisis. There were remarkably fewer articles than in 1973–74. The term "crisis" was seldom used. The reporting on supply and demand was not homogeneous but contradictory. As a consequence, different views of the situation were supported.
3. The press presented the situation mainly as a problem of oil price and not as a problem of supply to the Federal Republic of Germany. Reporting on prices was homogeneous and gave a distinct picture of the situation.
4. The press was late to recognize the impact of the political crisis in Iran on the supply of oil to the Federal Republic of Germany. They did not give a clear and distinct picture of the shortages of supply in February and March of 1979.
5. There was no panic reaction among the population. Consumer behavior was quite normal, as if nothing remarkable had happened. There was, especially, no increase in demand.
6. From points 1 to 5 one can draw the following conclusions:
   The fact that the press did not define the situation as a crisis of supply to the Federal Republic of Germany prevented the consumer from feeling concern over the supply. The perception of the situation by the consumer prevented an increase in demand which possibly would have resulted in a serious shortage of supply. The tendency of the consumer not to buy more oil products than normally may have been supported by the reporting of the press on price increases. The consumer may have tried to compensate for higher prices to a certain degree by lowering consumption. Both factors may have helped to overcome the effects of decreased importation in a way that had little influence on the actual supply to the consumer.

The comparison of the 1973–74 and 1978–79 situations can be summarized as follows:

1. In 1973–74 there was actually no shortage of supply to the Federal Republic of Germany. The press overestimated the impact of the decisions of the petroleum-exporting countries on the importation to Germany. The consumer believed the press and bought more oil products than normally. As a consequence, a shortage was created by the panic reaction of the consumer which confirmed the false picture of reality.
2. In 1978–79 there was actually a shortage of supply to the Federal Republic of Germany. The press underestimated the impact of the decrease in world oil production on the importation to Germany. The consumer, again, believed the press and did not buy more oil products than normally. This reserve was encouraged by the reporting on oil prices. As a consequence, the shortage in supply became invisible, which again confirmed the false picture of reality.

In addition to the short-term effects of the definition of the situation by the press which were analyzed here, there were also remarkable long-term effects. As a consequence of the 1973–74 experience, the German population widely supported the construction of nuclear energy plants. During the following years, the nuclear energy industry came under the attack of very active minority groups which had a strong impact on public opinion. As a consequence of the invisibility of the 1978–79 crisis, support for the construction of nuclear energy plants continued to decline. Finally, the construction of new plants was blocked up.

From this summary some conclusions can be drawn:

1. In both situations, the press gave a false picture of the supply.
2. In both situations, people reacted to the definition of the situation given by the press and not to reality itself.
3. The false picture of reality created by the reporting of the press had a negative effect in the first period and a positive effect in the second period on the short-term management of the situation. In contrast to that, it might have had a positive effect in the first period and a negative effect in the second period on the long-term solution of energy problems in the Federal Republic of Germany.

References

Archiv der Gegenwart, Vol. 50 (1980) pp. 22 160–23 474.
Bundesamt für gewerbliche Wirtschaft—Aussenstelle Hamburg— : Mineralölstatistik der Bundesrepublik Deutschland. Jahr 1979 mit Vergleichszahlen Januar/Dezember 1978; 1.–3. Vierteljahr 1979 mit Vergleichszahlen Januar/September 1978; 1. Halbjahr 1979 mit Vergleichszahlen Januar/Juni 1978. Hamburg 1979, 1980 (not in print).

Institut für Demoskopie Allensbach, Allensbacher Archiv

Kepplinger, Hans Mathias and Roth, Herbert: Kommunikation in der Ölkrise des Winters 1973/74. Ein Paradigma für Wirkungsstudien. In: *Publizistik*. Vol. 33 (1978) pp. 337–356.

Kepplinger, Hans Mathias: and Roth, Herbert: Creating a Crisis: German Mass Media and Oil Supply in 1973/74. In: *Public Opinion Quarterly*. Vol. 43 (1979) pp. 285–296.

Kepplinger, Hans Mathias: Paradigm Change in Communications Research. In: *Communication*. Vol. 4 (1979) pp. 163–182.

Schiffer, Hans-Wilhelm: Die Entwicklung der Mineralölwirtschaft in der Bundesrepublik Deutschland im Jahr 1978. In: *OEL-Zeitschrift für die Mineralölwirtschaft*. Februar 1979, pp. 42–46.

Schiffer, Hans-Wilhelm: Die Entwicklung der Mineralölwirtschaft in der Bundesrepublik Deutschland im Jahre 1979. In: *OEL-Zeit-schrift für die Mineralölwirtschaft*. Februar 1980.

World Oil Production. In: *Petroleum Economist*, June 1979, p. 261; May 1980, p. 225; May 1981, p. 228.

THREE

OPEC and the Western Press

Charles Snow
Senior Editor, Middle East Economic Survey

My topic is OPEC and its treatment in the western press. Since this is obviously a subject in search of a thesis, if not an entire book, I am afraid I must preface my remarks with a number of definitions and exclusions, in an attempt to pare down the subject to manageable proportions.

My comments are not intended to apply to the energy trade press, with its small circulation and limited impact on public opinion.* Nor am I qualified to deal with the "popular" press, where the very complex political and economic factors determining oil prices are invariably reduced to a question of how many cents more a gallon of gasoline is going to cost. My remarks, therefore, apply to what is called the "quality" press and, to narrow the subject yet further, the English-language quality press, including the international and national dailies (*International Herald Tribune*, *Times*, *New York Times*, and so on) and the up-market magazines (*Economist, Time, Harper's*, and the like). I must also say that, while time limitations force me to deal in generalizations, there have, of course, been exceptions, both honorable and dishonorable. Balanced comment has appeared from unexpected quarters, while publications which pride themselves on cool objectivity have, on occasion, gone completely over the edge when OPEC and/or oil is the subject.

* In any case the trade press is accurate. It has to be.

Within these limitations and as a generalization, I think it is fair to say that few, if any, of the major news stories of the last decade have been so egregiously and consistently misreported as the energy crisis and the shift in the balance of economic power from the oil consumers to the oil producers. The hostility which greeted OPEC's sudden emergence as an economic power in 1972-73 was, perhaps, understandable. Thirty years of abundant and cheap oil supplies had created the comfortable illusion that low-priced energy was an inalienable right in the industrialized countries, and disillusionment is always painful, particularly when it is expensive. It is less easy to understand, however, why the western media, almost a decade after the first oil shock, still appear to be unable or unwilling to grasp the realities of the world energy situation.

Perhaps the most depressing feature of the media coverage of OPEC is the dogged persistence with which the same misrepresentations continue to surface long after they have been disproved by events. Let us take as an example the contentious issue of oil prices and inflation. It has become almost an article of faith in the western press (and in the popular consciousness) that (a) oil prices have risen continuously since 1973, and (b) these price increases have been the main, if not the sole, cause of inflation in the industrialized countries. Neither of these "facts" is true. Following the oil price increase of 1973-74, oil prices fell (in real terms) by an average of 2.9 percent per annum over the four-year period 1975-78. By the end of 1978, consumer energy prices in Japan, Switzerland, and Australia were actually *lower* relative to other prices than they were before the 1973 Arab-Israeli war, and in the United States, Britain, and Germany they were no more than 15 percent higher.

These facts would almost certainly come as a surprise to the average reader of the western press. The truth about inflation might prove to be even harder to swallow. Data Resources Inc., an independent U.S. consultant, has concluded that in the United States, oil price increases contributed 0.7 percent to inflation in 1973, 1.6 percent in 1974, 2.5 percent in 1975, and nothing in 1976, 1977 and 1978. In 1979, when the average price of OPEC crude doubled, U.S. oil price increases were responsible for only 2.2 percent of the overall 13.3 percent inflation. I would add that since OPEC oil prices were frozen in nominal terms (and declining in real terms) for most of 1977 and all of 1978, there is probably an argument to be made that they were anti-inflationary in this period, a possibility which no one seems to have considered.

So when, for example, a U.S. President announces to the world (as President Carter did in January, 1980) that "all the increases for practical purposes of inflation rates since I have been in office have been directly attributable to OPEC oil prices," the OPEC countries naturally suspect that they are being used to deflect electoral resentment which would more properly be directed against the governments of the oil-consuming countries themselves.* They find the role of scapegoat all the more galling since the impact of the inflation exported to their economies by the industrialized countries has been far more devastating than the reverse effect of higher oil prices.

I have mentioned the connection between oil and inflation because it is one area where OPEC's claim to be misrepresented is quantifiable. But it is hardly the only area where the OPEC countries feel—with considerable justification, in my view—that they are hard done by. There is a whole series of half-truths and distortions about OPEC which have been promoted and repeated in the media so often that they appear to have gained an unshakeable hold on the public imagination.

Among the commoner manifestations of this mythology is the conviction that OPEC is Arab, despite the fact that six of its thirteen members—Indonesia, Iran, Gabon, Venezuela, Ecuador, and Nigeria—are not. This is particularly evident on editorial pages, where cartoonists regularly portray the oil producers as Gulf Arab. These cartoons are not only inaccurate in themselves but deeply offensive, since the stereotype they depict—fat, hook-nosed, sinister, and sneering—taps a vein of racist venom the likes of which has not been seen since the heyday of the Volkischer Beobachter in Germany in the 1930s. If these racial slurs were the only consequence of the identification of OPEC with the Arabs it would not perhaps matter very much in practical terms. But I hope to show below that this identification has, for a variety of reasons, served to hamper communication between oil producers and consumers at a time when everyone stands to gain from mutual understanding. In the meantime I must, in all fairness, admit that OPEC is not invariably portrayed in cartoons as an Arab. I have also seen it depicted as a snake.

Then there is the question of energy prices in the consuming countries. The routine assumption that OPEC alone is responsible for the high cost of oil products brings to mind a notorious ad for Renault cars which appeared in 1979. Entitled "How to make a Sheik Shake"—again the OPEC/Arab equation—it stated. "If the members of the oil producing countries hoped to get rich by putting petrol prices up to cover £1 a gallon they will be furious when they see the government mileage figures." Surely it is not too much to ask that some acknowledgement be made that the major component of the retail price of oil products is domestic taxation, which accounted for nearly 42 percent of the price of the product barrel in Western Europe in 1979, as opposed to a 28.4 percent share for OPEC?

The OPEC countries are not only greedy, they are also both rich and

* Assuming that President Carter believed what he said, it might also be argued that if he could not correctly identify the causes of inflation there was little hope that he could do anything about it.

mean. Rich because a small number of them (Saudi Arabia, Kuwait, Qatar, and the United Arab Emirates) have been producing more oil than they need to and accumulating large financial surpluses, and mean because they refuse to help the developing countries which have been hardest hit by the very price increases which have created this wealth.

It would be difficult to say which of these two allegations is the more aggravating and unjust. In the first place, whatever income the oil producers are at present enjoying is being generated by the sale of a wasting resource, and someone who is selling capital is getting poorer, not richer. Secondly, the OPEC countries as a whole, despite the high visibility of a small number of surplus states, are far from affluent by any accepted economic yardstick. Their collective per capita G.N.P. in 1979 was around $1200, compared to some $7400 in the OECD* countries.

The surplus countries themselves face special problems when it comes to their treatment in the western press. No sooner had they begun to accumulate funds than the specter was raised of an OPEC takeover of western industries with dire (but unspecified) consequences. Frequently they are accused, almost in the same breath, of threatening to buy up western economies *and* trying to ruin them with oil price increases, in which case they should fire their investment managers. The recent acquisition of Santa Fe by the Kuwait Petroleum Corporation—a deal that was endorsed by the Santa Fe board and highly profitable for the company's shareholders—has provided the latest opportunity for this kind of outburst. One headline I saw read "US Row Looms as Santa Fe is Grabbed by Arabs." I doubt whether this kind of language would have been used if the purchaser had been, for example, a German company. And again, behind the smoke screen a real issue is being obscured: if we want these countries to go on exchanging a valuable resource, such as oil, for an uncertain quality, such as the dollar, it would help if some reasonably remunerative form of investment could be found for their dollars.

The assault upon OPEC from the Third World angle is two-pronged. First, all the woes of the developing countries are laid at OPEC's doorstep and it is asserted that oil price increases are uniquely responsible for their problems. Then, the groundwork having been laid, OPEC is accused of doing little or nothing to remedy the havoc it has wrought. Perhaps it is because such assertions are unworthy of reply that they have remained so long unanswered in the western press, but I doubt it. It is patently absurd, if not hypocritical, to pretend that oil price increases have harmed these countries more than the soaring inflation in the prices of their imports from the industrialized countries, leaving aside questions such as the transfer of technology and the stagnant prices paid by the OECD for the

* Organization for Economic Cooperation and Development.

commodities which the Third World exports. As for aid, the OPEC countries would probably agree that not enough is being done. But they would also point out that in the six-year period 1973–78, they gave between 1.4 percent and 2.7 percent of their G.N.P. in aid annually, while the figure for the OECD countries never rose above 0.35 percent.

Lastly, in this brief review of the main themes of the anti-OPEC symphony, I would like to pick one which is much more prevalent in the United States than in Europe. It was ably summarized by Craig Karpel in *Harper's* in January 1979 when he wrote that "aside from OPEC there's no energy problem." The corollary to this assertion is, of course, that if OPEC can be made to go away so will the energy crisis, and we can all go back to filling our 12 m.p.g. cars with 40-cents-a-gallon gasoline. This is a dangerous, if comforting, fantasy. A recent study* estimated that without the OPEC price increases in the 1970s, world oil consumption would have climbed to nearly 80 million barrels a day (b/d) by 1980 rather than the actual figure of 49 million b/d. There is literally nowhere all that extra 31 million b/d could have come from. The message is clear: given the pressure of consumer demand on a dwindling resource, the energy crisis would have occurred whether OPEC existed or not. It is difficult to understand how anyone can, at this late date, believe otherwise.

This review of misconceptions about OPEC, which is far from exhaustive, is short on specific instances, not because of a lack of material, but because it would be invidious to choose from the wealth of sources available. To demonstrate that the OPEC-bashing school of journalism continues to flourish, however, I have chosen an article by Hobart Rowan which appeared in the *Houston Chronicle* on July 21, 1981. I would stress that this article was selected more or less at random, which is to say that it is only the worst example of its kind to have come to my attention in the last month or so. Entitled "Saudi Arabia can't do much about oil glut," it contains a number of misstatements about OPEC and the world oil market which, if unintentional, display ignorance, and if deliberate, malice. The first of these is that "the Saudis, as a matter of self interest, are optimizing their income from oil by producing 10.3 million b/d at $32/barrel—revenues they need to support ambitious budgets at home." Well now. Estimates by financial institutions such as the Morgan Guaranty and Chase Manhattan banks put the Saudi budget surplus that year at between $40 and $44 billion. A quick spell at the nearest calculator will convince anyone that at $32/barrel it requires some 3.4 million b/d to produce annual revenues of $40 billion, so the Saudis could obviously cut their production to 6.9 million b/d without even affecting their budget. Mr. Rowan is also apparently unaware that there is a considerable body of opinion within Saudi Arabia which is in favor not only of cutbacks in the Saudi

* By Texaco. See *Petroleum Intelligence Weekly*, August 10, 1981 p. 4.

development expenditures, but of reducing oil production at the same time to the level of the country's financial needs—5 million b/d being a figure frequently mentioned.

Next, Mr. Rowan asserts that the current oil glut has arisen because of "OPEC's excessive price increases in 1979-1980." This is a rather simplistic description of a period in which it was the consumers who bid up spot market prices while OPEC scrambled in their wake to raise official prices. Then, pausing briefly to equate the premiums paid by buyers in a tight market with bribes, Mr. Rowan moves to this coda: "The obvious fact is that OPEC can't sell all the oil it can produce at prices it would like to charge. That ball game is over." I have news for Mr. Rowan—that ball game has been over since 1973. The assertion that the objective of the oil producers is to sell all the oil they can is so wide of the mark that it causes one to question Mr. Rowan's qualifications to write about OPEC at all.

I would now like to investigate—again briefly and generally—some of the possible reasons for the sustained hostility towards OPEC displayed by the western press and western public opinion as a whole.

To start from a narrow professional perspective, I do not believe that oil coverage (and perhaps economic journalism in general) excites the same kind of professional interest as does, for example, foreign affairs. It is a subject that is at once dull, complex, and important—a combination of qualities with little to recommend itself to ambitious journalists. However, while it is true that there are very few specialists in oil writing regularly for the large circulation dailies, I do not really think this is anything more than a contributory factor. For the main causes of OPEC's treatment in the press, we must look elsewhere.

To state the obvious first, no one likes it when the price of a commodity as indispensible as oil—and one taken for granted for so long—increases so sharply and for so little apparent reason. This is the bedrock foundation of the sense of personal outrage that permeates most reporting on OPEC. Moreover, this sense of outrage is fueled (if that is the word) by the high visibility of oil in the consumer market. Every driver who stops at a gas station, and every householder filling his heating tanks is reminded regularly of the fact of high oil prices.

But again, I do not think this fully explains the sustained nature of the invective against OPEC or the way in which resentment against higher oil prices has spilled over to color attitudes towards almost anything OPEC does, be it recycling petrodollars or giving aid to the Third World. The roots of this phenomenon spread into wider areas of psychology, history, and, I am afraid, politics.

OPEC, as I noted above, has for whatever reasons been identified with the Arabs. To say that anti-Arabism is endemic in the west today is only to state the obvious. The result of this identification has thus been to focus a whole range of historical, cultural, and even religious antagonisms on

OPEC, which, properly speaking, have very little to do with oil. The origins and extent of the ill feelings between Arab and western civilizations are obviously so far beyond the scope of this paper that I will not even try to examine them here.* However, any explanation of the reaction in the west to OPEC which does not take this element into account would be inadequate.

A second effect of the OPEC/Arab identification has, of course, been to involve the issue of OPEC with that of Palestine. This means that a good deal of what is written about OPEC in ostensibly economic terms is in fact politically motivated and, therefore, polemic. The Rowan article I have cited is a case in point. The arguments, however weak, are economic. But the unstated and a priori objective to prove that Saudi Arabia is doing no one any favors, is political, and it is obviously related to the recent debate over the sale of AWACS aircraft to the Saudis. This kind of camouflaged political attack is less common in Europe than in the United States, where vociferous popular support for Israel has encouraged both the politicians and the press to use OPEC as another stick with which to beat the Arabs. The least that can be said is that this has done little to clarify the economic issues involved.

In the face of this onslaught, OPEC as a collective entity has reacted along more or less conventional lines. Ministers tour, spokesmen speak, handouts are released, and publications are distributed. It has even established its own news agency, which it views as part of the wider effort to promote a more balanced coverage of Third World affairs in the western media. All this seems to me to be based on the rather endearing belief that it is the availability of the facts that is the problem, and that if these were only more widely known OPEC's image problems would be solved. I mean no discredit to the OPEC Information Department when I say that its efforts have done little to change the biased coverage of OPEC in the western media. Frankly, given the very wide range of animosities that have coalesced around the issue of oil, I doubt there is much anyone can do. It is quite possible that the only course open to OPEC is to wait it out until the passage of time weathers its image and it becomes an accepted, if unwelcome, feature of life.

Lastly, does it matter? Has the successful depiction of OPEC as an irrational group of alien extortionists whose monopoly of a vital resource is a threat to the economic health and moral rectitude of the industrialized world had practical consequences? Or to put it more crudely, would things have been any different if OPEC had received a better press?

The answer is only maybe. One cannot say that the press has any direct influence on governments. However, it does form public opinion, and

* *Orientalism*, by Dr. Edward Said, (Panthcon Books, New York, 1979) analyzes this cultural collision elegantly.

public opinion in the western democracies in turn defines the range of options available to governments. Given that hostility towards OPEC is a political fact of life in the consuming countries, and given that OPEC is portrayed and perceived as an adversary in everything it does, these options have, in the last decade, been pretty much narrowed down to one: confrontation. To illustrate this I need only quote a memorandum prepared for President Carter in the summer of 1979, when his standing in the opinion polls was plummeting. The first recommendation of an eight-point program to restore the president's popularity was to "mobilize the nation around a real crisis with a clear enemy—OPEC."

The irony is that if anyone has been harmed by the creation of an atmosphere of confrontation, it has not been OPEC. No one is maintaining that there are not sharp and lasting differences between the oil producers and oil consumers. But this should not be allowed, as it has been, to obscure the fact that they also have interests in common. The failure is one of perception, and perception is a function of the press. The Renault ad I referred to earlier described the oil producers as "shaking with rage" because "everyone buying a Renault is going to be saving petrol and money." This, it concludes, "wasn't what the Sheiks (sic) had in mind." But it was exactly what the oil producers had in mind, as even the briefest scrutiny of statements by OPEC officials would prove. The producers want to stretch the life of their oil reserves. The consumers wish to decrease their dependence on OPEC and improve their balance of payments. Conservation is a common objective. Yet the achievement of this objective is still being presented in the press as some kind of victory over OPEC.

This is not the only point where real as opposed to perceived interests coincide. Two other areas where both sides could cooperate are in maintaining real oil prices at a level that will ensure the development of the more accessible alternatives and in facilitating the flow of investment from OPEC into the industrialized world. OPEC for its part has always been more willing than the consumers to recognize that such areas of common interest exist. Indeed as far as consumers are concerned, one can only speak of an almost wilful refusal to recognize any areas where cooperation might be more beneficial than confrontation. How far the treatment of OPEC in the western press is responsible for this state of affairs may be open to debate. What is not debatable is that OPEC has yet to be accorded anything like a fair hearing for its side of the case.

FOUR

Oil Coverage: A Discussion

Nelson Smith
Leonard Theberge

Like the assassination of Archduke Francis Ferdinand in 1914, the stock market crash of 1929, and the invasion of Poland in 1939, the Arab oil embargo of 1973 was an act which ignited a world crisis. Imposed as a political weapon against the United States and other countries supporting Israel during the Yom Kippur War, the embargo announced a new economic reality: dependence by industrialized western nations on the critical resources of Third World states.

For Americans, the embargo was devastating in two senses. First, it crippled their national economy, affecting their own daily lives more dramatically than any event since World War II. Second, and perhaps more damaging, the embargo further undermined the American sense of well-being already reeling from the Viet Nam War. It was a confrontation for which there seemed to have been no warning and no preparation. A sense of confusion and impotence permeated the American national debate which was absent in other industrialized nations. The proposed solutions — rationing, price controls, and allocations — echoed the programs of wartime, and yet here, there was no victory to be won from a malevolent foe. Here, there could be only adjustment and accommodation to the reality and demands of a new age.

To understand how swiftly things had changed, one need only be aware that the Arab states had attempted the same tactic six years earlier, when the United States had extended similar support to Israel during the Six-Day

War. In the 1967 episode, however, the impact was negligible. At that time, imported oil made up only 21.1 percent of American supplies, with OPEC's Arab members contributing a fraction of that amount.

By October of 1973, a radical shift had occurred. U.S. crude oil production peaked in 1970, while consumption continued to climb. American dependence on overseas oil had increased dramatically in those six years. When the second embargo struck, imported oil made up 36.4 percent of U.S. supplies, and, most significant, half of that total came from OPEC countries.[1] The embargo itself, and the consequent quadrupling of prices by OPEC members, had an immediate impact on the U.S. economy. Eventually, everyone who drove a car or heated a home—virtually everyone in the country—felt the chill.

Spiralling energy costs, plunging thermostats, and disruptions of daily routine were visible evidence of an extraordinary realignment in economic power. Beneath the clashes in Congress and the street-corner debates lay another stratum of expectations and beliefs which suddenly seemed porous and weak. In addition to the incongruity of having American economic policy decided in Riyadh and Vienna, fundamental precepts such as economic growth and corporate profits were challenged.

Americans, who had grown up listening to tales of industrial miracles, who knew their farmers fed the world, suddenly began thinking of themselves as consumers, critically dependent on someone else's production. Consumption, previously a virtue, came to be stigmatized. The world was treated to images of overstuffed Americans, 6 percent of the planet's population, gobbling 30 percent of its oil supply.

In cannot be said that any one sector was particularly well-prepared for this onslaught of political and cultural change. The government reacted with an array of bureaucratic programs and public relations ploys such as the continuation of price controls, the creation of a Federal Energy Office, and the launching of a massive campaign entitled "Project Independence" which would, it was claimed, free Americans from dependence on foreign oil by 1980. None of these was effective in ending the crisis. Conservation, increased U.S. production, and movement toward alternative fuels came about as the result of higher prices. OPEC price rises and the decontrol program, begun in April 1979, ended the crisis.

The oil industry was caught off-guard. Oil executives who had boasted of their companies' profits were now required to explain them in an apologetic tone of voice. Like any enterprise, the oil companies had done well by getting people to buy more of their product; now they were forced to urge conservation. When shortages developed, their chiefs were paraded before congressional committees, where, for politicians, reporters, and the public, they were easy targets in appearing to benefit from the shortages. But a more telling example of the industry's disarray at this point comes from a CBS News interview in which an independent gas station owner complained that one of the major companies was trying to force him out of business: "I work hard to sell their products. I don't think it's fair."[2]

If government and the oil industry were unprepared for the energy crisis, it should come as no surprise that the press was, too. Prior to 1973, energy was treated as a subject for the business columns, or as an adjunct to environmental stories. The three television networks had no special arrangement for energy coverage. Aside from the occasional story on oil import quotas or the Alaskan pipeline, television displayed little interest in energy. Such matters as price controls and import levels were acutely non-visual and lacked audience appeal.

Energy became a headline story overnight—probably *the* headline economic story of the decade. Press coverage started from the ground up. One network correspondent tells the story of how he wound up on the energy beat: his producer walked into a roomful of reporters and asked if anyone knew how many gallons to a barrel of oil; the reporter who came the closest got the assignment.

If the United States was jolted by the 1973 embargo, and its institutions and people were rudely awakened to a new set of circumstances, how did other nations fare? One may think of the energy crisis as an ongoing phenomenon, but at least with regard to oil, there seem to have been two distinct periods of difficulty. The first was the winter of 1973–74, encompassing the Arab oil embargo and the initial OPEC price inceases. Western economies experienced a recession in 1974 and 1975, partly as a result of these events, and so there followed a period of relative stability in oil price and supply that lasted until late 1978. The Iranian revolution caused a shutoff of their oil production and that shortage, coupled with the second round of OPEC price increases in 1979, may be thought of as another discrete "oil crisis." Throughout these two periods, America had a difficult time adjusting to the economic forces at work. Other major industrial powers, much more dependent on imported oil than the United States, were more adaptable.

According to Dr. Hans Kepplinger (Chapter Two) the West German response appears to have diverged sharply from the American reaction. In West Germany, government and industry seemed to have had adequate supply in the first crisis, while the press overstated the dimensions of the problem, thereby "creating" a crisis, in Dr. Kepplinger's phrase, by artificially stimulating demand. In the second crisis, press treatment of a real oil shortage, due to West German dependence on Iranian oil, was more reserved, inhibiting the type of panic buying by consumers which had occurred in 1973–74.

Other western industrialized countries also experienced sharp controversy over the policy options available to meet the new economic realities. However, they had no gas lines; they did not attempt to keep oil and gasoline prices controlled at artificially low levels comparable to those in the United States; and they had long ago embraced the ethic of efficiency in automobile driving and other energy-consuming activities due to the relatively much higher prices than in the United States.

The range of issues discussed at Ditchley Park gives one an idea of the breadth of oil/energy journalism in the 1970s: the "conspiracy theory" (Did the oil companies manipulate supplies for their own profit?); the secretiveness of the oil companies regarding pertinent information; the transition from abundance to scarcity in oil supplies; the role of government in resolving or exacerbating the crisis; and the interaction of reporting and government policy.

In the sessions at Ditchley Park, Americans shared their experiences with colleagues from Europe and Japan, contrasting the strengths and weaknesses of different media cultures in dealing with complicated issues. In the following pages, some of the discussions and conclusions on coverage of oil issues are recounted, along with a commentary to place the discussions in context.

The Conspiracy Theory

> If you visited an American news organization in the 1970s, a fellow did feel a bit as if he was in a victorious Indian tribe after Little Big Horn. "We've got the Watergate scalp of the President of these United States on the saddlebag of the press. Geronimo!" — Norman Macrae

Most accounts of the oil crisis have overlooked the extraordinary political climate in which the first crisis (1973 – 74) took place. The Arab oil embargo struck two-thirds of the way between the Watergate break-in and the resignation of President Richard M. Nixon. Government credibility was severely strained. When a worldwide military alert was ordered on October 24, 1973, in response to the threat of direct Soviet intervention in the Mideast conflict, many Americans believed the alert to be a maneuver designed to distract attention from the Watergate affair.

According to one study of CBS News energy coverage in that period,

> [T]he same impatient, doubting approach taken by those investigating the Watergate affair was taken by senators such as Jackson, Percy, Ribicoff and Proxmire, who played media coverage of oil industry hearings for their full political value . . .
>
> On January 21, 1974, for example, seven chief executives from America's largest oil companies were shown with their right hands up as they were sworn in before the Senate Antitrust and Monopoly Subcommittee. The camera panned the panel of Senators and focused on Committee Chairman Henry Jackson (D-Wash.) who said, "People want to know why the price of heating oil and gasoline has doubled when oil companies report record high inventories." Without showing the executives' response, the camera showed Sen. Charles

Percy (R-Ill.), who said, "We're in a hell of a mess." Next Sen. Arabham Ribicoff (D-Conn.) said, "I believe we have as much gasoline today as we did a year ago, but the public is so scared that you've changed their pattern of buying."[3]

The fact that the overcharged atmosphere of Watergate contributed to suspicion of major oil companies does not explain or exonerate their behavior in the crisis of 1973-74. As we shall see below, there was intense and perhaps justified criticism of their secretiveness in furnishing information. However, Watergate certainly helped set the scene for a prolonged period of baseless charges against the oil companies.

Watergate created another problem for those involved in establishing energy policy. The political scandal instilled in the press and public a macabre interest in uncovering national scandals. When oil shortages hit and energy prices zoomed, the natural inclination of journalists and the public was to assume someone was once again up to dirty tricks. Unfortunately, this simplistic tendency to look for a villain obscured the causes of the crisis. The complex historical and economic events which led to the shortages were never explained or understood.

Authors Robert Stobaugh and Daniel Yergin, citing polls in September 1979 showing 45 percent of the American people unaware that the United States imported *any* oil, said:

> This simple ignorance, in turn, has contributed heavily to the search for a domestic villain on whom to blame the problem. The adversary character of the American political system, the never-ending welter of charge and counter-charge, the regulatory confusion, the cacophony of contradictory expert opinions—all of these reinforced the tendency to go on an energy witch-hunt.[4]

In discussions at Ditchley Park, participants returned often to the political environment in which Americans first confronted an energy crisis. They found in it a partial explanation for the emergence and persistence of a "conspiracy theory"—undocumented charges that the oil companies had contrived shortages and manipulated supplies in order to reap "obscene" profits. In the following comments, participants examine the development and discrediting of this theory, in its various guises, in the several nations under consideration.

NORMAN MACRAE: Where the press went terribly wrong in '73-'74...was the ghastly conspiracy theory. There was a witch-hunt on Nixon, which turned into a witch-hunt on big oil. I give a slight excuse to the press on this, though. The economic situation was that even before the oil price increases, we were getting into an inflationary recession because of the money supply increases in every country in '71-'72 Suddenly you had this increase in oil which took about 2 percent of gross world product out of spenders' pockets and into OPEC savings, making demand less, inflation higher, balance of payments worse. You needed very considerable political sophistication around the world. In the two biggest economic powers of the free world—Japan and America—you had conservative heads of state; unfortunately, at the time, all the papers were saying that both of them ought to be in prison . . . . So there was a hell of a political situation occurring then.

HERBERT SCHMERTZ: I think that the criticisms some of us made of press coverage in '72 and '73 in part generated the backlash of the conspiracy theory—if the press was going to be criticized, then it would retaliate . . . . The one item which was most damning to the oil companies in that period was the story about tankers lurking offshore. If you will recall, at that time the airline pilots, tugboat captains, everybody who could get out there saw hundreds of tankers lurking offshore waiting for higher prices. No report from the Coast Guard, the Department of the Treasury, from anyone else, could refute the myth . . . . The other most damaging item was coverage of the Jackson hearings, about which I'll offer an observation. I watched Irving R. Levine of NBC the night of the first Jackson hearings, and his report is imbedded in my mind as the perfect example of television's emotional reporting. He opened by saying, "In the same room where the Watergate burglars were testifying before a congressional committee . . ." It was the Senate Caucus Room. He could just as easily have said, "In the same room where John and Robert Kennedy announced their candidacies for the Presidency of the United States." But he chose to couple the oil executives with the Watergate burglars, and we can all surmise what the viewer came away with—Watergate, oil companies, they're all crooks.

JEFF GREENFIELD: The Watergate aspect of the timing of the first oil crisis seems critical to me because the embargo hit almost simultaneously with the "Saturday Night Massacre." So the official government—which Alan Reynolds says is treated credibly in terms of statistics—was in fact being treated as felons in the dock . . . . Numbers that were coming out, statements being made, were being treated as though coming from unindicted co-conspirators.

WILLIAM D. SMITH: I divide the coverage of that era into three categories. You had the Malthusians, the people who believed we were running out of oil and wrote their stories accordingly. They paid attention to numbers and facts. They may not have always been right, but they were looking at it from a hard, factual point of view. You had the Machiavellians, where black is never black and white is never white, and there is conspiracy all over the place. The third group I call Glickians, after Sammy Glick, the lead character in the play *Sweet Smell of Success*. He would do anything at any time to ingrain himself with the aura of success. The American press, during both the '73-'74 crisis and the '78-'79 crisis, had a lot of Glickians. They wrote to the galleries. It seems to me that the conspiracy theory is tied to the Glickians, appealing to the worst in the American public. It's not quite show-biz, but it is an attempt to half-entertain, and it has resulted in confusion.

HANS MATHIAS KEPPLINGER: In West Germany, during the first period, we had a conspiracy feeling in the press. Not all, but most of the press believed that the international oil companies and OPEC had created a major, official shortage—and this was presented as the result of a conspiracy. This was not the case in the second period. There was no serious statement on that topic then, not one.

FRANÇOISE MONIER: Before 1973, energy writing had a very small audience in France, and then all of a sudden in '73-'74 the press took the very emotional side of what had happened. Shortages made very long front-page stories, but coverage was not focused on supply, demand, or reserves. Rather, the newspapers feared an attack on the privilege of driving cars—a very superficial sort of coverage. There were two conspiracy theories in France. The first was about oil companies and the second was about Arab countries, which lasted longer than the first. The Arabs were accused of putting their new money into European economies, with some sinister ideas in mind.... Eventually the reporting improved in quality—but people still wanted to hear sensational stories and that's probably why the best reporters preferred not to stay on the daily newspapers, but to write books.

NORMAN MACRAE: I think people got a bit ashamed of both overstating the shortage, which didn't exist, *and* of the conspiracy theory. When '78 came around, the press *under*stated the shortage and the conspiracy theory had become less of an issue—the politics had swung to the right.

ADRIAN HAMILTON: I don't think you need very complex questions about the conspiracy theory. The problem for any nonspecialist reporter is that he naturally wishes to seek some kind of quick, independent assessment of things. So he naturally hesitates to trust those who seem to him to be too self-interested—and is therefore naturally a dupe for either believing (as was the general perception at the time) that governments tend to hold some objective truth, or that outside consultants, outside economists, themselves hold some truth. They look for a quick source that will give them some kind of balanced judgment. The reason why the conspiracy theory has fallen apart is less a perception of truth, I think, than the simple fact that the oil companies' control of supply, therefore their role in answering questions on the topic, is a great deal less than it was in those days....

JEFF GREENFIELD: You also have to go back beyond '73, I think, to understand this phenomenon. Maybe it's just an American characteristic, but the willingness of people, at least in the United States, to believe all kinds of conspiracy theories is endemic. I was raised in a family that was reasonably well-educated, many of whose relatives are convinced that there was a light bulb which would last forever, only the electric companies had bought it and were keeping it in a closet; that there was a pill you could drop in the gas tank which would make water into gasoline; and that there was a midget that wrote all of Irving Berlin's songs. We needn't get into the Kennedy assassination theories which the overwhelming majority of Americans believe. I'm suggesting there's a fertile climate which can't be blamed on any one reporter.

* * *

If people believed there was a conspiracy, they also believed they were not getting enough information. Soon after the 1973 embargo struck, the quantity and quality of information on production, reserves, and supply of oil became a prime focus of national attention.

According to *New York Times* correspondent Edward Cowan,

> Two types of issues concerning information emerged from the embargo. One was a complex and subtle question about how to read the data—whether high stocks of fuel, for example, amounted to significant evidence that the shortage was spurious.... The second was the reliability of information available to the government about oil production, imports, and stocks. That data came weekly from the American Petroleum Institute (API), a trade association.[5]

At first, suspicion about false data centered only on industry, and the 1974 legislation creating the Federal Energy Administration (FEA) directed the new agency to begin assembling a variety of statistics. By 1976, however, a new concern had arisen: FEA advocacy of energy policies might taint its information-collecting processes. Accordingly, Congress created an Office of Energy Information and Analysis, separate from FEA's policy-making apparatus, and that bureau was later incorporated into the Department of Energy as the Energy Information Administration.

Despite all the care given to developing reliable energy data, however, there remains in the United States a great residue of distrust about the oil industry. A November 1979 poll published in the *New York Times* found half of the respondents believing that the oil companies had contrived the energy shortage. It is revealing to compare this tally with the results of a Louis Harris survey (February 1981) of general public and selected opinion leaders in Great Britain. Sixty-three percent of the public, and 66 percent of the leaders, claimed "a great deal or quite a lot of confidence" in the oil industry as a source of information on energy matters. There is a vital difference between the two countries with respect to energy, of course. North Sea oil has made Great Britain energy independent and helped to keep the nation afloat in the perilous economic seas of the past few years. The industry might even be regarded a bit heroically.

The questions remain, though: did the American oil industry help or hurt itself by the way it treated energy data, and by its relations with the press? And did the press function responsibly in portraying industry policies on critical information?

HERBERT SCHMERTZ: The myth oil companies are secretive—that was certainly true 30 years ago, 20 years ago perhaps. It was certainly not true in 1973 and it is certainly not true today.

JAMES C. TANNER: I disagree. Up until '73, the oil companies were not only secretive, they were downright arrogant. It was a public-be-damned attitude. It was very difficult to cover oil companies. I remember not too many years ago having to get a proxy—a stock proxy—to get into an annual meeting of one oil company. Now, there has been a big change in the energy companies, but that change has occurred since 1973, since the finger was pointed at them.

JEFF GREENFIELD: Some of the skepticism about the oil industry was coming not from left-wing public interest groups but from members of the Nixon administration, whose conservative credentials were absolutely indisputable. In fact, the first official I can find who raised the issue that the oil companies were simply not coming clean with the numbers was William Simon when he was "Energy Czar." He was quoted in that left-wing publication, the *Wall Street Journal*, on January 18, 1974, saying that oil company information simply wasn't adequate, and that he, as "Energy Czar", was demanding more . . . . It you want to talk about the press picking up conspiracy theories: in late '73, one prominent figure misread an API [American Petroleum Institute] study and told a press briefing that producers, the oil companies, were blackmailing consumers for higher prices. It turned out he had simply misread the paper. That fellow was Alan Greenspan.

My point is that if reporters, faced with a subject of enormous complexity that they have never had to think about, turn not to Jane Fonda, but to William Simon and Alan Greenspan, and are being told (a) that the oil companies are withholding information, and (b) that there is indeed a conspiracy to withhold supplies until the price goes up, one can't assert that bias is at the heart of the problem.

ALAN T. GREGORY: I would say the oil industry has a lot to answer for, because before 1973, they were exceptionally non-communicative. And in the case of my own company, for example, the Achnacarry Agreement* was a thing one simply didn't speak about—although it was at that time a necessary piece of economic management in a slump—something seen as perfectly normal for the industries then, who were indeed making similar arrangements with the help of concerned governments.

MICHEL ANFROL: In 1973, when the crisis started, I was covering the story in Washington and New York, and I still remember very well the lack of cooperation from the oil companies. And when, with my crew, I wanted to go to some parts of Texas or California to do some filming, every time, I almost got arrested by the private police because we were taking pictures of oil fields.

JAMES C. TANNER: In '73, when there was a need for real experts of some sort, well, you could go to a petroleum engineer and find out why a certain

* Representatives of British Petroleum, Esso, and Shell of the Netherlands met at Achnacarry Castle, Scotland, in 1928, to set prices for world oil markets.

well did this or that—but in terms of hard data there was nobody around without axes to grind. You could go to an oil company, to a Walter Levy, or to a politician, but in each case there was a certain axe being ground, a certain sphere of expertise being exercised. Charles DiBona, who is now president of API, was Nixon's first "Energy Czar," and he admitted that he knew absolutely nothing about energy in that very critical period when he was first hired. He learned fast, he's a good man, but there was really nobody around that one could talk to and get a full grasp of what was going on.

*   *   *

It would be misleading, however, simply to print selected comments arguing that governments and oil companies did or did not present "the facts." Such is the complexity of oil supply that two experts seldom agree on objective reality, whether it is expressed by a corporation or by a government.

In order to illustrate the continuing difficulty of achieving agreements on the facts of energy policy, additional sections of the Ditchley Park transcript are reprinted below. These deal largely with the nature and scope of shortages; with the gravity of the individual crisis periods; and with governments' role in "creating" crises. Keep in mind that these discussions took place eight years after the 1973 embargo. In light of the wide discrepancies they present, one wonders whether a coherent view of the crises of the 1970s will emerge before the next century.

WILLIAM D. SMITH: I think something that has been often missed in reporting energy—because reporters don't have the time to do it—is that the United States was coming from a different angle. We were the only nation with all the "goodies." We had never experienced shortages, except during wars, and suddenly out of nowhere we're being told we don't have enough energy. And a typical American reaction is not to solve the problem immediately but to blame it on someone—and we had two ideal candidates: the Arabs, those funny people in white garments, and the oil company fat cats.

ISABEL MUHLFENZEL: I must disagree with Dr. Kepplinger when he says there was no real crisis in '73. I think there was the biggest crisis ever; there was an *intellectual* crisis. In the years before, we had all talked about the affluent society, everything was great, consumers spending a lot and so forth, and suddenly in '73 - '74 the idea came that there was a shortage. And, in my opinion, this was a real change; it started a new area of thinking. It has not so much to do with actual supplies or shortages, but I think it explains why newspapers and TV people like myself reported more on this subject in '73 and '74 than in '78—because by that time people were used to the idea of shortage.

MICHEL ANFROL: I think that foreigners in the United States knew that something was bound to happen, since with about 5 percent of the world's population, the United States was consuming 33 percent of the world's energy. Some kind of crisis was going to start, someday, in the United States.

ADRIAN HAMILTON: Americans have been brought up to believe, partly through government action and partly through life in America, that the U.S. is isolated from international developments. For anyone who has covered economics on the international level. America has been enormously selective in understanding the international ramifications of things—the question of international interest rates, international currency flows, and so forth. Most people had been brought up without the need to understand these things. So in the energy crisis, the difference between the European and American press reflected, to a large degree, the fact that in Europe, everyone had been brought up familiar with shortages. I mean, my sweets were rationed as a child, in the post-war period. And Europeans had all been brought up to regard oil as an international thing, because at that stage very few countries had indigenous hydrocarbon resources. Americans had never had to go for very long without butter, or anything else.

ANTHONY J. PARISI: I would stress, though, that there were, indeed, crises in both 1973-74 and in 1978-79. And, they weren't just political or intellectual. There was a physical shortage of oil in both instances, and the data makes this pretty clear. The shortage was small and the panic that the reporting may have set off may have exaggerated it, but there was an actual, physical short-age. And the fact the price rose attests to that. I mean the fact is, a shortage is an economist's artifact. He posits a shortage, then he sees a price rise. As the market clears, the shortage isn't there, so there was no shortage—that's the logical sequence. But really, the price went up to close the gap, and the shortage went away because of that.

HERBERT SCHMERTZ: Tony's right; there was a small gap between what the public wanted and what the oil companies were able to supply in both periods. But the gap was not nearly as bad as the lines at the gas stations in both '73-'74 and '79 would have justified. Every country around the world experienced essentially the same shortfall because supplies were balanced, but only the United States experienced the terrible problem of the long lines. The story that the press missed—continues to miss—is that the lines were caused not by the small shortage but the ridiculous allocation program that the government adopted, which forced oil companies to put supplies where they weren't needed and prevented them from putting them where they were needed.

ROGER PETERSON: It's not correct that there were no stories on the DOE (Department of Energy) regulations that led to shortages. For example, I had done two or three, and then the *New York Times* had a report, and I was asked to do another story, and I said, "I've already done that story." There *were* stories on government regulations; the problem is, when you do a story, you consider it done. We're not conducting an editorial campaign—we don't keep hitting the same stories over and over again.

NORMAN MACRAE: It's true that in '73, if you were a journalist and knew when the price went up that there was going to be a glut of energy. This incredible reporting was all over the papers saying there's a desperate shortage, rationing forever. But I don't agree that it was entirely the press's fault—at least not in my country. The government in our case was helping to create a panic by giving us rationing coupons which of course we'd never use. I wrote "Sell your coupons now, there isn't a shortage." And in January there was an article, "The Coming Glut of Energy," which I still think was right.... I think the '78 crisis was a very much bigger one than the bogus '73-'74. I really believe this, with 4 million barrels a day disappearing. The press at that time, in Great Britain too, made an undercall, partly because of the shame of over-reporting the shortage of '73-'74. And somebody like me says, "For God's sake, this is a real crisis," and they say, "What on earth are you panicking about? You were one of the ones who got it right in '73-'74; my God, you *do* jump about all over the place!"

ALAN REYNOLDS: Several times we've talked about the *two* oil crises or shortages—they're not shortages in the common sense but reduction of supplies—and I think this is another one the media have failed us on. There have not been two crises; there have been three. The third crisis was Iran-Iraq, which was every bit as important as the Iranian revolution in terms of its impact on OPEC supplies. The reason it wasn't reported is that it was anticipated; there was a lot of stockpiling in anticipation of it, and therefore it didn't have an immediate effect. It did have a delayed effect in the United States and I guess elsewhere, too. And when we began to see the effect, then it was, of course, attributed to the decontrol of oil, which is demonstrably incorrect. The absence of reporting of a third oil shock that is every bit as important as the other two is really rather bizarre.

*   *   *

A central consideration of the Ditchley Park conference was the relationship between media reporting and public policy. In the television age, the constant flow of information between government and constituents has made that relationship kaleidoscopic, and has posed new challenges for the bearers of information. Lloyd Cutler, former counsel to President Carter, has written, "Television has probably amplified the power of the bully pulpit, but it has also shortened the time span of power; few television performers can hold their audience for four consecutive years."[6]

With most of the population having been weaned on TV, it's not surprising that the national attention span has been truncated. Whether television and the press in general are at fault, or whether more intricate causes were to be blamed, the public's weariness of energy issues began to stifle the policy-making apparatus. Citing the puny accomplishment of the Natural Gas Policy Act of 1978 and its ratification after long months of debate, Stobaugh and Yergin noted: "The effort to get even this much had been an exhausting one. Energy Secretary James Schlesinger compared this first major legislative effort to Mao's Long March. There was a general weariness about the energy issue, especially in view of growing doubts about the existence of the threat. And the meagre result after 18 months of heated debate struck foreigners both in producing countries and in other oil-consuming countries as a discouraging indication that the United States was simply not capable, in terms of public attitudes and perhaps of institutions as well, of coming to grips solidly with the dimensions of the energy problem."[7]

Four and one-half years passed between the onset of difficulties in 1973 and the passage of the Natural Gas Policy Act (NGPA). To make a wholesale indictment of media performance in that time would be to overstate the case; certain sectors of both print and broadcast media acquitted themselves well. But in some cases, the instincts, education, and habits of journalists defeated their attempts to promote understanding. Why, for example, did CBS News devote only *one sentence* during the entire embargo period to explaining the Federal Energy Office's two-tier crude oil pricing policy?[8] One suspects that there was little bias involved in that editorial decision, but rather, that its significance was simply beyond the understanding of the program producers, whose orientation in any case was toward more lively, visually arresting pieces. It is highly likely that in this important instance, the medium defeated the message. And since price regulations continued throughout the seventies to be an astounding source of economic misunderstanding, it is also likely that early editorial failures like this one contributed to the prolongation of the energy wars.

What, then, was the interplay between reporting and policy? Both sides of that equation were represented at the Ditchley Park sessions, and their exchanges follow:

ROBERT S. GORALSKI: I think it was in March of 1975 that the European Economic Community came out with a report asserting that the shortages of 1973-74 were not contrived. One of its recommendations was that the multinational oil companies be encouraged to diversify, go into other fields using their knowledge, expertise, and money. And I believe it was within 30 days that there was a U.S. Senate committee which came within one vote of trying to break up the American oil companies. You had a very dramatic demonstration of different perceptions being translated into public policy. The reaction was the direct result of how the public perceived the '73-'74 crisis on two continents.

TOM BETHELL: One thing that did result was the sudden discovery by the press that the U.S. had no "energy policy." And this in turn was translated into the discovery that we didn't have a department of energy. So DOE was indirectly created by price controls. The controls created a shortage, which created the perception that there was no energy policy, which created the

Department of Energy. Of course, all along, the U.S. *did* have an energy policy: the allocation and distribution of oil and gasoline by price.

HERBERT SCHMERTZ: I'd like to take the issue of profits in terms of bad national policy resulting from the dialogue between government and press. I'm convinced the misreporting of profits was not started by politicians but was started by journalists who just weren't competent or who didn't want to know a rational way to report profits, particularly quarter-by-quarter increases. It is very rare that you see profits reported in terms of return on equity, return on assets, or in the traditional measures used by people who make investment decisions—as a percentage of sales, or any other index that makes sense. They are reported quarter-by-quarter, in percentage terms or in sheer dollars, both of which are meaningless. And it was the press, in my opinion, that started the misreporting and misconceptions on the part of the public about the profitability of the oil companies.

In 1973 and even today, it's hard to find journalists who understand the difference between profits and profitability. The politicians saw what was happening in terms of the reporting of profits, and saw a terrific horse to ride— not only Senator [Henry] Jackson with his "obscene profits," but no less than the President of the United States [Carter] was riding this horse. And the result was that in '79, when there was to be crude oil decontrol, the President was able to send up a piece of legislation calling for a so-called windfall profits tax. I visited almost every United States Senator during the period, and the vast majority said, "Yes, I understand why this is bad legislation, but there's absolutely no way, considering how it is appearing in the press, that I can go back to my constituents without doing some damage to the oil companies. When you can get public opinion back on your side, come back and see me."

JEFF GREENFIELD: Reliance on government officials as a source of information, which Tom Bethell's study on inflation for The Media Institute illuminated, is not the same thing as saying that consumers of news believe it. I think that is a mistake which runs in a lot of media content surveys . . . . Perhaps the most interesting evidence of that, although you may not think it conclusive, is that after these two crises in which the oil companies got beaten about the head and shoulders, President Reagan and many of the Senators we elected—well, to describe them as hostile to the oil industry is stretching the case. So you have to keep in mind that the public discounts much of what it hears. And the fact that a government official is trying to excuse government incompetence, and that's a report on the network news, doesn't mean either the journalist or more importantly the public accepts it.

BEATRICE LACOSTE: In France, the written press certainly had an impact on the population, both in terms of blaming OPEC for oil prices, and also in terms of having nuclear power accepted. But as for the impact of the press on policy-making, it was really the other way around: policy-making influenced the press.

MICHEL ANFROL: Well, I don't think that television in France influenced either the government or the public. Sometimes, a newspaper can bring about some kind of new law with a few reports and a few letters to the editor—but speaking of oil prices and energy, I don't think television changed anything . . . . What's missing in this discussion is the news agency. I think the reason so many newspapers and networks covered the story as they did was that they got the story day after day from United Press International (UPI) or Associated Press (AP) or Agence France-Presse (AFP). I know very often, in our reporting, we get something on the wire, and we'll send out a team, and they are just asked to get some kind of illustration of what is on the wire. I think that maybe the news agency had more influence on energy coverage in 1973 and 1974 than any newspaper by itself, or any American or French network.

ROBERT S. GORALSKI: I've always been impressed by the fact that the American motorist refused to believe there was an energy problem; part of this is obviously that he thought it was contrived. The fact is, until the price explosion of '79, the Cutlass Supreme—eight cylinders—was the most popular car built in the United States. We went through a period when, as consumers, we simply refused to take conservation seriously. The problem wasn't real in anyone's mind, and therefore since it was contrived, it wouldn't last forever. And only when you had the final crunch of '79 did people go to small cars. So conservation took hold, but contrary to what the public had perceived as the problem.

WILLIAM D. SMITH: Right after '73–'74, Detroit came out with smaller cars, and the U.S. government's failure to price oil at the higher level meant that no one would buy the damned things. Oil pricing in that period contributed to the subsequent decline of the U.S. auto industry.

JOHN F. O'LEARY: I'd like to cite an example of influence working both ways between politicians and media. After the presentation of the national energy plan in 1977, the congressional reaction carefully cultivated by the hawks, among whom I count myself, was that conservation was not enough; you needed supply incentives. In the spring of 1978, President Carter tacitly agreed to a significant increase in the budget for supply initiatives. We then began a quarrel in the media between the hawks and the doves on energy that ran all through the summer of 1978, both sides attempting to plant their own view of the future. The hawks took the view that the Middle East was unstable and that further upsets were inevitable; the doves took the view that stability was guaranteed and that surpluses of energy would characterize the future, rather than shortages, and consequently there was no need to move forward. In retrospect, the doves won hands down.

At that point, shortage discussions in the newspapers were not news. The hawks were unable to plant a great deal of attention-grabbing material. But the people who came out and said that the energy crisis was over were able to command space in the newspapers and thus able to influence opinion. In

December we came to the final test. The Shah was about to decamp, and production had already been closed off briefly two months earlier. We went to the President with these two opposite views, and the President, buoyed by public support for his view that conservation was really the road to follow, that you didn't need supply initiatives, that in the final analysis the Middle East was a secure source of supply, reneged on his promise of the spring. And of course, when things went wrong, during the winter of 1979, he turned again, because of public opinion. So quite clearly the interplay here ran both ways. Politicians influenced the media—but indeed, the media influenced politicians.

NORMAN MACRAE: I do think the oil companies themselves didn't sufficiently state that price decontrol is the answer. I think they were defensive. On the whole, Europe was shouting "America should decontrol its prices," more than even spokesmen for the American oil industry.

*   *   *

Finally, the panelists had several comments on the training of journalists and their values, and on the cultural environment in which the decade of oil crises took place.

TOM BETHELL: Reporters in general have been trained to think that getting information from an oil company spokesman is a violation of the First Amendment. Nevertheless, these reporters often did not understand the most basic principle of ecnomics. What was missing then—and I believe is still missing—was any understanding of the role of price in equalizing supply and demand. If you artificially hold the price down, then you get shortages, as Mr. Parisi pointed out. But these journalists, who were consorting almost exclusively with government officials, failed to point out that price controls had been created by government, and that these controls had a disastrous side effect. They produced an illusion of shortage, which was taken to mean that we were running out of oil. It became very hard for journalists to understand that such an untoward outcome could have resulted from what appeared to be such benign intentions. So I think it is the failure to understand the price mechanism which is by far the most important problem in media coverage.

ROBERT S. GORALSKI: Something very significant happened in '73-'74 in terms of television reporting. I think the television networks collectively decided that the energy issue was simply too complex to cover, and there weren't people who understood it. And a decision was made to report it in terms of the consumer. In order to make it understandable, we'll talk to the guy in line, or we'll talk to the person or family *in extremis*, where the spot will start off, "John and Mary Smith both make $125 a week. Last month their electric bill was $85." There was a direct rule we got at NBC to cover stories in terms of understandable consumer impact. And great was the day when we discovered a family of six living in a Victorian house, uninsulated, and they couldn't afford to turn on the lights or the television, and they were sitting there in the dark. This was a particularly good story. Everybody loved it. High impact. And you see this kind of thing in the programs every night—big, complex stories are reduced to the plight of the family. It's bound to have an effect on somebody in Washington who has got to legislate some way to get that television set back on for that family.

JEFF GREENFIELD: If there's one bias that television has, and it cuts across everything it does, it is the bias toward the personal. Television is just much better at dramatically bringing into our homes the plight of an individual than it is in debating abstractions, which are words. Nobody in television knows how to translate abstractions into pictures, and for television you need pictures. When you go out to do a story, whether it's somebody in a gas line or somebody affected by a real estate operator converting apartments into co-ops, the easiest thing to do is to find a victim, a person the viewer can identify with, and put that person up against a major enterprise—the oil company or whoever it is.

ALAN REYNOLDS: The relationship of economic magnitudes—for example, the relationship of the value of the dollar to the dollar price of oil—is rarely mentioned.

ALAN T. GREGORY: In the case of oil companies, we have a problem that we are so big, we have become the centerpiece of issues that really have nothing to do with oil. A classic current case is the argument in the U.S., and even in the U.K., on the diversification of my company (British Petroleum). When people say that it is wrong for oil companies to get into coal or minerals, they're not really talking about oil companies. I suspect they're talking about a suspicion or mistrust of large, multistream, multinational companies, the sort of which an oil company is the natural example.

JAMES C. TANNER: When the '73 embargo began, editors and publishers wanted to find out what was going on, wanted their reporters to win a few Pulitzer Prizes. They did rush a lot of untrained reporters in to cover energy. I recall some of the questions I heard; for example, one magazine called Exxon and asked, "How many barrels of oil do you move in a day?" The answer was something like 4 million barrels. "Well, isn't the real shortage in barrels, not oil?" But the media mirrors our community. Not so long ago I heard of a stockholder letter coming into Exxon asking, "Why did you build so many service stations on every corner if you knew there was no oil under them?"

DAVID KELLEY: I wanted to make a point about polls. I have an article from *Public Opinion Quarterly* which summarizes a CBS/*New York Times* poll on whether the shortage was contrived or not.[9] And in '79, you get figures in the 63–69 percent range. But there are reasons to be skeptical of the poll itself. Listen to the exact question: "Do you think the shortage of energy we hear about is real or are we just being told there are shortages so oil and gas companies can charge higher prices?'' Now, these things are matters of judgment, but it sounds to me like they're looking for a cynical answer . . . . One other point, which illustrates a difference between the U.S. and Europe: The energy crisis quickly became much more of a moral issue than an economic issue, so far as profits are concerned. In the press and in popular opinion, there is a kind of hostility toward the profit motive as something quite selfish. And it's reflected in the fact that, by the time the windfall profits tax was passed, it was quite clearly a punitive measure, not really designed to be of any economic value. The moral attitude seems to be this: the profit motive is basically dubious because it's self-interested. As a "necessary evil," it has to be constrained by two things: One, the profit has to be fair, it has to be earned, which is really an issue of justice; and two, it has to be clearly in the public interest—which is an end-oriented consideration. I think there was a great tendency to see the increases in price, and the increases in oil company profits, as something that was not earned. And, therefore, you could make any economic case you wanted that the market had to regulate through the price mechanism, and it wouldn't matter—because the issue had already been framed in terms of justice.

Notes

1. Department of Energy
2. Robert Okun, "The Energy Crisis and Television: A Study of The CBS Evening News and the 1973 Oil Embargo," The Media Institute, 1981, p. 26.
3. Ibid., p. 28.
4. Robert Stobaugh and Daniel Yergin, "Energy: An Emergency Telescoped," *Foreign Affairs* 58, no. 3 (1980); 586.
5. Edward Cowan, "Problems With Government Advocacy: A Journalist's View," *Informing The People*, ed. Lewis M. Helm et. al., (New York: Longman, Inc. 1981), pp. 46–47.
6. Lloyd Cutler, "To Form A Government," *Foreign Affairs* 59, no. 1 (Fall 1980): 138.
7. Stobaugh and Yergin, "Energy," p. 567.
8. Okun, "The Energy Crisis," p. 22.
9. Al Richman, "The Polls: Public Attitudes Toward the Energy Crisis," *Public Opinion Quarterly* 43, no. 4 (Winter 1979): 576 ff.

PART TWO

Nuclear Energy Coverage

FIVE

The French Press and Nuclear Power

Françoise Monier
Senior Correspondent, L'Express

Beatrice Lacoste
Free-lance Journalist

An Industrial Venture Turns into Gallic Nationalism

In France, the nuclear energy debate has always been influenced by the military origin of the nuclear industry. It is no wonder that nationalism is a major argument in favor of it, as was the case for French military defense. And it is not surprising that nuclear energy opponents are suspected of lacking a sense of patriotism.

A confusion between nuclear weapons and energy is made all the more natural by the fact that the French atomic bomb was built under President de Gaulle, and it was he again who chose the first industrial process to develop peaceful nuclear energy in France. The identification with the military was made even more emphatic in 1973, when France experimented with atomic weapons in the Pacific. At that time *L'Express* was still vehemently anti-Gaullist and it launched a vigorous campaign against the country's atomic weapons.

Françoise Giroud seized the opportunity to write one of her most stunning editorials:

> Within a radius of 3 km all life is thoroughly annihilated. Within a radius of 5 km, lungs explode.... Who, knowing that, can accept without shame, that a curse be put on the name of France.

The titles of subsequent articles squarely opened up the battle: "Shame," "A Terrible Blunder," and "Stop Everything." The leading theme in this

79

campaign was the following: "The French atomic weapon is not powerful enough to give us the total independence it was initially supposed to." (Jean-François Revel, Editor of L'Express)

Apart from *L'Express* and the communist papers, most of the press supported the nuclear experiments. After all, nationalism lives on. This theme was ever present in all nuclear reporting in the pro-government press until the fall of Giscard d'Estaing. The following statement made by Giscard when visiting Pierrelatte in August 1977 truly rings of Gaullist grandeur: "Nuclear energy is at the crossroads of France's double independence: the independence of her defense and the independence of her energy supply."

Energy policymaking remains somewhat colored by this military attitude. As a senior reporter in the economic press puts it, "Some of us wrote as though we were in the middle of a war. Perhaps this goes back to 1914 when Clemenceau had a fit of rage because Exxon refused to sell fuel for French tanks."

The first big debates on nuclear energy took place between 1967 and 1973. At stake was the choice of the industrial process—French or American; Westinghouse or General Electric; Compagnie General d'Electricite or Groupe Schneider. According to the press, France had embarked on a great industrial venture, engaging in the battle between big firms and crusading for industrial chauvinism. During this period, the press seldom questioned nuclear power as a source of energy. The fuel was accepted as the best economic source, even on a long-term basis. The press never assessed the far-reaching consequences implied by the choice of nuclear energy—be they social, political, or economic. Nor did it consider the problem of safety.

When the American nuclear process was chosen, one of the well-known editorialists of that period, Gabriel Farkas, wrote in *France-Soir* of March 28, 1969, explaining that giving up the French process meant that France "would not only be out-distanced by the Americans and the British, but also by our European neighbors, the Germans, the Dutch, and the Swedes." Nationalism had found a new field of action. The economic daily, *Les Echos*, urged on October 22, 1970: "It is absolutely imperative that the French industry be present when it comes to nuclear electric production." And it quoted the Industry Minister: "We must strengthen our grip on the domestic and international markets."

A few weeks before the 1973 oil shock, an official report suggested a very ambitious program for nuclear plants. In the report's highest estimation, by the year 2000, 85 percent of electricity produced in France would come from nuclear energy. This staggering percentage did not seem to put anyone off. Indeed, *Les Echos* vauntingly announced: "Nuclear plants will become a tremendous industrial venture." And when they mentioned the risk factor, they referred only to the financial gamble. The economic monthly *L'Expansion* insisted: "Up to now, the nuclear industry has come across endless desert."

The 1973 oil shock and the appearance of OPEC on the world stage only served to exacerbate this nationalism. One must bear in mind that France was still licking its Algerian wound and that it was highly sensitive when it came to Arabs. So OPEC could only be seen as Arabic, and Arabs could only be viewed as scoundrels who wanted the downfall of Western economic systems and especially the French economic system.

Public opinion had more down-to-earth preoccupations: it feared a rise in the cost of fuel, a rationing of gasoline, and all kinds of restrictions. When Pierre Messmer, Prime Minister at the time, presented a plan to cut down on oil and develop nuclear energy, newspapers commented more on the former. Heating and driving made the big headlines, as did, of course, speed limits on highways. The nuclear part of the program went down very smoothly. "The main Government objective is to by and by reduce the country's energy dependence from abroad," commented *The Monde*, sternly. The atom was seen heroically coming to the rescue of an endangered France and thus it symbolized the country's vitality.

The press, ever obedient, reported the Prime Minister's speech on television: "No other country in the world, apart from the United States, has undertaken such an effort." *France-Soir*, a widely distributed morning daily and the most popular Parisian newspaper at the time, launched a series of major reports entitled "France Needs 200 Atomic Plants." The choice of nuclear energy appeared as a great "success story" from a scientific, industrial, economic, and even human point of view. The drawbacks were described as the inevitable counterpart of any adventure.

In May 1974, Pompidou died, and France, in the midst of its presidential campaign, paid practically no attention to the nuclear issue. All the candidates, except for the ecologist candidate, generally agreed on the great lines of French energy policy. *Le Monde* was the only paper that gave the reason: public opinion is only aware of the Arab oil embargo and the limitations it implies. "When the embargo came to an end, the problem became almost exclusively a question of price and income, that is to say, it was left to the experts."

Not surprisingly, during all this time the most chauvinistic and pro-nuclear articles were found in the communist press, particularly in the daily *L'Humanite* and the weekly *L'Humanite Dimanche*. The communist press took up the three favorite themes of the Parti Communiste Française (PCF) nationalism, the fight against multinationalists and America, and the defense of industrial progress. For the red press, communism is electricity plus the Soviets, and nuclear electricity seems better than any other. On September 9, 1980, *L'Humanite* cried out indignantly:

> The future of French nuclear energy is threatened .... We are seriously worried about our future independence so far as energy is concerned .... Let us remind our readers of the strategic importance of nuclear technology in which France is the world leader together with the USSR ... the future is there! Our future, for it means we could become self-sufficient in our uranium supplies.

Passion and Policies

The Messmer Plan was accepted without any real protest. France became involved in the nuclear game and the general press welcomed it, even when the government went on to the next stage—the building of fast-breeder reactors. The first small prototype, "Rhapsodie," did well and a second reactor, "Phenix," was also a success. The press exultingly published the news bulletins released by the Atomic Energy Commission (CEA). *Le Monde* in April 1977 asked with a mixture of pride and anguish: "Super-Phenix: A Nuclear Concorde?", fearing that, like the Concorde, the Super-Phenix would be cold-shouldered by the Americans and left in splendid isolation "although it represents the peak of nuclear research, because industrial credibility is at least as important as technical efficiency." Gaullist grandeur was ever present, and author Jean-Louis Lavallard concluded, "Thus France may find itself leading, but alone." Very few papers discussed future risks and foreseeable problems. Articles dealing with liquid sodium cooling systems or the transport of plutonium were invariably confined to scientific sections.

The idea of nuclear proliferation was seldom linked to the building of Phenix and the other fast-breeder reactors that would follow. The journalists dealing with the proliferation aspect of nuclear power were foreign policy experts who considered themselves as members of a superior caste. Very little was written about such crucial problems as available uranium resources, both in France and in neighboring countries. The press was very selective where the "African Connection" was concerned.

On May 16, 1977, *Le Nouvel Observateur* tersely commented on the war dangers of a nuclear bomb brought on by the French-developed enriched uranium process in an article titled "Uranium, the French Bluff." It stated: "The huge publicity operation set up by the Elysee and conned by the French Atomic Energy Commission was aimed at boosting Valery Giscard d'Estaing's prestige at the London Conference where the seven richest Western countries were to meet." Fabien Grukier went on to criticize the secrecy with which Andre Giraud, at that time head of the Commission, had surrounded the project. Very sparing of technical details, Andre Giraud had only volunteered that "it was a chemical process" and Grukier exposed the absurdity of the "bluff." Giraud stated, "And this plant would simply be made up of big containers in which uranium crystals would float about. As harmless as laundry, instead of these mechanical and electrical monsters that are normal enrichment plants . . . it would take little more for the atom thus described to be as pleasant and enjoyable as local Asian or African crafts."

It is well to recall that *L'Observateur* was an opposition paper at the time. When in July 1977, ecologists announced plans for demonstrations in Creys-Malville, on the site chosen for the fast-breeder reactor, Super-Phenix, the press mentioned it—but without giving it any more importance than other ecologist demonstrations against dams or military settlements (Larzac). It was a summer routine! *Le Matin* was the only paper to produce a comprehensive article before the demonstration entitled "Why Phenix Is Feared."

The demonstration of July 31, 1977 came as a shock to France. A few press representatives were there, those who usually cover ecologist demonstrations. A violent clash broke out between the police and the demonstrators. One protester was killed, scores were wounded, but above all, there were civil war scenes. The next day, all the papers had front-page headlines in print as big as the Yom Kippur War headlines. *France-Soir* on August 2, 1977, after the Creys-Malville killing, announced in huge type, "Bonnet, minister of the Interior, speaks in accusation." The story went on to say:

> Action groups of anarchist tendency (1,000 out of 20,000 demonstrators) have deliberately trespassed the limits and attacked the police forces.... The socialists of the area denounce the brutality of the repression and condemn the acts of violence of the demonstrators.... Perhaps there is a nuclear policy problem. But we shall refrain from deciding one way or the other except by referring ourselves to the know-how of scientists. But there is a political problem: that is the mode of expression that passionate groups feel entitled to choose to make themselves heard....

It was the turning point. As the *Monde Diplomatique* put it, "A crisis often screams out denouncing the working mechanism of a social system in a much more acute way than a normal situation would." The outbreak would remain at the political level in the press. It was a dramatic, bloody happening, making huge headlines, but nobody bothered to look into the real issues at stake. Why did all of this happen?

"They have no right to use this death," newspapers indignantly cried out when a political debate started up between political groups. Headlines were brazen. Stories exploded with the sound of hand grenades and bloodshed. The real issue was more or less forgotten. Papers of the opposition took advantage of the happenings to attack the government or even the whole system. For *Liberation*, the small leftist daily, it was a field day. In one sweep, it lashed out against the police, the prefect (a symbol of centralized authority), nuclear power, and capitalism.

For the first time the "nuclear" state and the "police" state were identified as one: On August 11, 1977, *Le Monde* published a reader's letter:

> I am an average Frenchman, peace loving and law abiding. I think I am representative of millions of my fellow citizens. Malville was the first fascist and military blow dealt openly to democracy. It is the beginning of the civil war that awaits us if the left wins the elections in 1978....

Liberation printed: "Nuclear society and the police state became one, whereas only several months before they had been two distinct nations." And, hoping that Creys-Malville was but the first step, the paper went on to say: "It was the first real mass movement on this theme in France and it became an effective political force." But as it turned out, Creys-Malville was not to be followed by more bloody demonstrations.

Nevertheless, a few in-depth articles were published. A journalist from Agence-France Presse felt that this major event "broke the silence of the press . . . . We could send off stories on waste recycling, proliferations, alternatives. The press picked them up, whereas it would not have before."

But it was all to no avail. The fundamental debate never really took place. Consequently, when the Three Mile Island accident hit the press, it was an unexpected catastrophe. Again, passions flared up, and the political rift in the media widened. On the one hand, anti-nuclear journalists in the anti-government press described the accident as a major catastrophe that could happen in France. On the other hand, the pro-nuclear group in the pro-government press wrote that, in fact, nothing really important happened, and that, at any rate, in France there was no such risk.

One of the most brilliant journalists on French television, Francois de Closets, wrote in August 1977 an editorial published in *L'Express*, which said in part: "The nuclear debate will be swallowed by the polemic dilemma before it even gets launched. Catastrophe is fashionable. Atom phobia could find its place between the Club of Rome Report and the film 'The Towering Inferno.'" It is a fact that the press asked few questions on the fundamental issue such as the role played by the hydrocarbons or new energies. Most journalists accepted government figures on the cost of the nuclear kilowatt per hour, without criticizing the short life span of nuclear plants, the lack of assessment of risks, or the effective cost of stocking or recycling nuclear wastes.

A Little Democracy, Please!

Toward the end of the 1970s, a new era had begun in which the nuclear energy debate centered less and less on economy and safety, and increasingly on the share that citizens might have in the decision-making. In 1978 in Great Britain, the press gave wide coverage to public hearings on the enlargement of the Windscale recycling plant. Few French papers picked it up. "A debate that should also be held in France," simply commented *Le Matin*. Also in 1978, an Austrian nuclear referendum attracted little coverage. Two years later, things changed a little as the media gave a similar Swedish referendum wide coverage, although its main motivation was to threaten a conservative government (in the case of Windscale, the London government was not involved as such). Nevertheless, the French had been surprised to see that a debate between pro- and anti-nuclear forces could rock the country of Sweden for months. But on the whole, the French media gave it less coverage than did the German or Anglo-Saxon press.

Certain papers—the opponents—began to reflect on the "nuclear society," and for the first time the word "nucleocrat" appeared. Who were the nucleocrats? They were that influential group of men in the government, the agencies, and industry who decided what France's nuclear future would be. Were they feared or admired? The press did not investigate their methods or their motivations. On the contrary, in *L'Express*, on May 18, 1979, a very flattering description was given of Andre Giraud, who the ever-rebellious *Canard Enchaine* called "the greatest nucleocrat ever in France," and who was, at the time, Minister of Industry after having been an impressive head of the CEA. *L'Express* portrayed Giraud as "Mister Atom, a little something of Clark Gable," with a taste for the flamboyance, the deep roots, the ambitions, and the instinctive reactions of the Gaullists. Giraud declared, a little in provocation, but mostly out of conviction: "I am the premier ecologist in France."

More seriously, several papers said that a society in which the main energy source is nuclear is a society where democracy is severely curtailed. On March 22, 1980, *L'Express* published an editorial by Olivier Todd, then editor-in-chief, who explained that he has met atomic engineers who are perfectly democratic:

> Nuclear energy is a highly complex issue—beyond the grasp of the people. And the government knows what's best for them .... Nuclear opponents bring up the fact that Austria, Switzerland, and, this very week Sweden, have held referenda. Perhaps the referendum makes democracy very like demagogy.... Even if schools had provided special classes on nuclear physics and economics, would 35 million voters be able to take an intelligent decision on this incredibly complicated issue?

And yet a village rose against the nuclear state and the press. In giving voice to a small revolution, it felt compelled to question the whole nuclear strategy. Plogoff, a little village at the far end of the Coast of Brittany, is peopled for the most part by women (most of their husbands are fishermen in the merchant marine) and the elderly. Plogoff refused to take part in the local Public Inquiry that the government had set up before building a nuclear plant in the area, although the deputies of the region had accepted. As in Creys-Malville, the government sent in police forces, because (and this was hardly ever said by the press) it was obsessed with the example of West Germany, where very active and powerful ecologists had effectively succeeded in paralyzing the nuclear program. But the violence of the clash at Plogoff spurred the press with more impetus than an ecologist demonstration could have. An Agence-France Presse journalist stressed: "The Plogoff coverage was more important than the Three Mile Island. It lasted longer and had a more dramatic impact." Finally, it focused public attention on the nuclear issue. "When I arrived in Plogoff," recounted a *Le Matin* reporter, "and when I saw these women and these old people face to face with the police—even when I heard their rather mythical arguments, I understood why they were fighting. The fact is, they felt they were being raped. I thought: 'This goes beyond the nuclear plant. Democracy is at stake.[1]'"

Nevertheless, the press was divided by politics. On the one hand, the conservative *Figaro* explained the "blind and burning passion" of the angry seafarers in Plogoff by "a resurgence of ancient primitive awe" and "a daunting fear that is irrepressible and carefully kept alive by the ecological lobby artistically blending so-called scientific arguments and Christain references to peace and human dignity." On the other hand, *Liberation* tried to capture the lyricism of Victor Hugo when describing the resistance of the villagers: "The shadow of Kaboul streches across Cape Sizun .... The village must unite against the invader...."

What use was all this reporting? After the Creys-Malville events, the government, E.D.F., and CEA agreed to devote a little more consideration to security. After Plogoff, it admitted half heartedly that the country needed more dialogue. There was not enough investigative reporting fundamentally to change the official strategy. Maybe the impact was elsewhere, in the people's minds. Even if the press never challenged the government's policy, its effect on public opinion was one of the many factors leading voters to change the leadership of the country in May 1981 while expressing anti-nuclear sentiments and a demand for more democracy.

Has it changed today? For the first time, the government recently organized a huge debate at the National Assembly on energy. The press covered it very thoroughly, with lengthy articles on the event and the background, and with interviews of pros and cons. Even TV organized debates with explanatory films. Never was the French press so good on energy. How long will it last?

The Way We Worked

In the course of the past ten years, energy coverage has been undergoing a slow, but steady, change. But let us quickly run over some of the major problems an investigative reporter writing about nuclear energy runs up against. To begin with, a journalist dealing with nuclear issues tends to have a general background. Usually he is either a reporter with specific scientific training (usually space exploration), or an economist with experience in the field of industry. Sometimes, he may be an environmentalist and, in that case, prejudiced against nuclear energy.

While the British have quite a few journalists specialized in foreign relations working successfully on energy problems, the French tend to have few. Consequently, they usually feel handicapped by their lack of technical and scientific expertise. French journalists are inclined to quote engineers or officials without challenging the accuracy of their statements or the soundness of their reasoning. Because of this lack of rigor in the non-specialized reporter, engineers and scientists are reluctant to talk to journalists for fear of being misquoted.

There are two main sources of information. One is official: the government, the E.D.F. (Electricide de France), the CEA, and so on; the other comes from various parallel movements dealing with energy: associations, such as Friends of the Earth, political movements, unions, and the like. Both of these sources have to be checked and that is often a formidable task.

The government and industry benefit from much more powerful means (see the Quiles Report at the end of this chapter). A conservative journalist has mentioned what was called the "Guillaumat attitude" (Guillaumat was a high official in the '70s): "One talks to journalists but one does not like them, and if they ask embarassing questions or write unpleasant things, they don't get invited back." He adds: "There is no technological counter power proposing valid arguments against the nuclear. The scales lean in favor of official sources. Otherwise we would be glad to print controversial information."

Engineers are also not free to talk. Yves Legal, a marine biologist interviewed in the March 1980 *Nouvel Observateur* stated in an article entitled "Plogoff: The Falsified E.d.f. Files": "I am beyond threats but scientists need E.d.f. . . . even public organizations or university labs depend on contracts with E.d.f.; if they talked they could lose their jobs." E.D.F. has the monopoly on research, and certain projects are funded by it 100 percent.

Another way to get information, of course, is to go and see for yourself. But a journalist's expense account is often meager, and he often gets to go only to places when he is invited. E.D.F. has organized lavish weekends at Chinon, Saint Laurent des Eaux, Fessenheim, and Le Bugey, with charterfuls of reporters invited to visit nuclear plants before lunching in style at a post restaurant. The company has found that by inviting the editors-in-chief, its propaganda action is more efficient. Unlike reporters, they do not write what they have seen and heard; but they do make sure that the stories published in their newspapers will be slanted to show E.D.F. projects in a favorable light. Hence, one comes across lyrical descriptions of nuclear plants as the cathedrals of modern times!

One must also recognize the more or less subtle pressures within the paper itself. "Censorship exists of course," says the editor-in-chief of an energy and environment monthly. "No information is ever objective but stories are not slashed with a cutter—they are seldom spiked. Censorship begins with the source of information, the obstacles set up in checking it, and a general diluting of significant facts or events."

The more an energy source is centralized, the less freedom there is for the individual who finds himself linked to the government. No energy source is as highly centralized as nuclear energy and most papers in France have decided to be either for or against it. In France this centralization is even greater than in other western countries, for there is only one electricity company and it is public. Obviously the journalist has no alternative but to side with his paper's choice. It would be pointless and quite mad to try and go against the general current. So the journalist may well decide to adopt an ostrich-like stance: he does not actually misinform, but by keeping certain things quiet, he succeeds in avoiding a clash.

Several sensational nuclear stories barely found their way into the French press. Why was that? Was it because they were happening outside the country (and were less interesting to an egocentric public opinion)? Or were the editors afraid that they would spark new controversy over the issue of nuclear safety? Whatever the reason, very little was reported about the Karen Silkwood story, "The China Syndrome," or the loss of plutonium needles in Great Britain.

As for television coverage, it has been very disappointing on the whole. A *Canard Enchaine* journalist exclaimed: "When Elkabach was appointed to the head of Atenne 2, he told me 'You'll see. We'll have five debates on the nuclear.' In fact, we only had one and it was not much of a debate."

Although there will always be secret ties linking the press to powerful lobbies and local oligarchies; although journalists will still tend to be prejudiced, openly announcing that they are pro- or anti-nuclear energy, newspaper owners will always try to prevent journalists from taking skeletons out of the closet. One must also stress that the press has been just as biased, whether it was pro- or anti-government, or pro- or anti-nuclear.

There is hope yet. The recent extraordinary thawing of tensions in the press is significant. For the first time, the media may seize the opportunity to become an effective counter-power, thereby forcing people in government to be more responsible and forthcoming in their own presentation of information.

Prudence, Pride

Flamboyant but reverential, cocksure and yet gullible, the French journalist covering energy issues all too often appears like an armchair quarterback arguing with the officials but seldom out on the field.

French energy coverage reflects the very efficient, highly centralized and monolithic French technocratic system. Official sources of information are seldom questioned, and the reporter is very likely to make up for his lack of investigative aggressiveness by a tendency to moralize and editorialize. Stories lack the pragmatic touch, and the real issue becomes lost or diluted in over-emotional political comments artfully hiding an absence of economic and technical expertise on the part of the writer.

But there is another side to the energy press coin. The heavy hand of the publisher is ever present in the newsroom, and out of frustration, those journalists who do unearth relevant material often feel compelled to pass along a scoop to the only French paper prepared to publish it—the *Canard Enchaine*.

The country's change of government is having a tremendous impact on the media, but it is hard as yet to say what will come out of the present turmoil.

Several of the influential papers interviewed for this account, no matter whether they were left, conservative, or ecological, had the same reaction to the 1973 and 1979 oil shocks: they welcomed them. Henri Lauret, of the daily *Le Matin*, explains:

> In a sense we tried to use the oil crisis and the rise of gas prices at the pump to make people realize there were all kinds of significant factors beyond the cost of gasoline, beyond the cost of their well-being. Television tends to oversimplify, showing spectacular events, and commenting in a very superficial way. Le Matin has always tried to present the complex chapters of the geopolitical game hidden below the glamour and the glitter of official international meetings.

Whereas most of the media in France joined in harshly criticizing OPEC, there were a few exceptions: the left-wing *Le Matin*, the *Canard Enchaine*, the *Sauvage*, and the conservative *Expansion*. Interestingly enough, they all mentioned ethical reasons for going against the general current. Quoting Lauret of *Le Matin*:

> It was difficult to make people understand what OPEC stands for. The government hesitated between two attitudes—either taking a dramatic stand and using OPEC as a scapegoat, or pretending that thanks to its brilliant leadership the government had everything under control, unlike other countries such as the U.S. for instance. We have always deliberately given OPEC a favourable image, for ethical reasons. Of course, there are countries such as Saudi Arabia where the wealth is tremendous for a very small population, but we have refused to picture oil sheikhs coasting out of Regine's or the casinos on the Riviera, their wallets exploding with petrodollars. Instead we have shown that OPEC also stood for poor countries—desperate countries in need of the bare necessities of life, that had been unfairly exploited for the past sixty years.

Lauret comments on how *Le Matin* covered the nuclear energy policy:

> At first we felt very critical of nuclear energy—mostly because of a lack of information, a lack of understanding. I think that today, all of us in this paper fully appreciate the implications of electronuclear power. In fact, we're not really better informed today, but what with the oil crisis, the absence of nuclear accidents, the fact that the nuclear does provide a lot of jobs at a time of severe unemployment, and that we are ahead in the field and derive considerable prestige, we have come to accept it as a necessary evil. We really try not to be biased and to give the pros and cons. Today the treatment plant at La Hague is the last bastion in the fight against the nuclear. But I do not think that there are ten engineers in France who actually know the whole nuclear file, so when it comes to journalists, who tend not to specialize enough, they naturally tackle the problem more from a political angle than from an economic or technological one.

Alain Murcier of the business magazine *L'Expansion* says:

> It is unfortunate that the press in France does not try to exert more influence on the government. Why doesn't it? Well, it is not very courageous I suppose, and then the press is rather lazy; it tends to be slack, not rigorous enough. Although it has improved over the last ten years, it still lacks scientific and technical expertise.

Taking this into account, what is the relationship between the journalist and the scientist or the engineer? Murcier answers:

> Journalists always tend to trust engineers. Reporters take it for granted that they are competent, that they know better, that they are serious, reliable people . . . . I tend to act like that myself. Of course there is a danger in the sense that the acceleration of the nuclear program increases the risks . . . but people are lulled to a state of comfortable trust. Journalists do not go out and investigate—they do not challenge the information that they are given because they do not feel competent.

The nuclear "debate" sheds a lot of light on the structures of power in France and on the philosophy that the state is based on. According to Alain Murcier:

> Now we accept the nuclear as unescapable. Up to ten years ago the nuclear was never attacked. Then there was this irrational psychosis, that was difficult to control because it came from fear and ignorance. The Peon Commission made up of scientists and politicians never found any opposition. The government never set up a mechanism of auto-criticism. In France the nuclear party is more powerful than in any other industrial country, made up of businessmen pushing for economic growth. They own the newspapers. Instead of working on a balanced, even development of alternative energies, the oligarchy tend to put down big packets of money on one or two spectacular projects, and as the press is the voice of the oligarchy, papers lead on big flashy projects that flatter their chauvinism. The Concorde, the Super Phenix are typical examples.

Murcier commented additionally on the debate over centralization in nuclear decision-making:

> Imagine what would happen if terrorists, wanting to destablize the country attacked a goods train carrying fissionable matter. The nuclear industry is so centralized that it is terribly vulnerable to acts of sabotage. If there were such an act of terrorism the police reaction would be incredibly violent. Another threat is the maze of high tension cables that criss-cross the country. We have called our readers' attention to it, but on the whole, the press hopes for the best but does not prepare us for the worst.
>
> Centralization of decision-making, knowledge, and information as it exists in France cuts both ways: authorities can exercise a strong sense of leadership and implement a nuclear or a solar policy efficiently, enabling the country to get way ahead in those fields. The government can also shut down voices of protest that explode in other countries such as the U.S., Sweden, or Germany, where decentralized communities have been initiated and where their ability to criticize and discriminate has been kept alive. In this country, people are not realistic—they don't want to pay bills, they don't want to face what things really cost, so they procrastinate, and inflation soars. The press takes on the same ostrich-like stand. We are not very democratic and the government would never risk losing a referendum. The philosophy of leadership in France stems from the notion that there are tremendous undercurrents of anarchy and that centralization is the only way to keep the country together.

> In a sense, you could say that the *Canard Enchaine* acts as a safety valve . . . if it did not exist, perhaps other papers would feel compelled to be a little more courageous and to speak up.

One can only regret that Albert Camus, the brilliant novelist, playwright, critic, and editor of the Paris daily, *Combat*, died without following up his idea of a "control newspaper" that would come-out an hour after the others with estimates of the percentage of truth in each of their stories and interpretations of how the stories were slanted. According to Camus, the idea was to keep an up-to-date card index system of paper owners and journalists. The interests, policies, and idiosyncrasies of the owners would equal "Z"; the prejudices, quirks, and private interests of the journalists would equal "Y". "Z" times "Y" would give you "X" — the probable amount of truth in the story. "But do people really want to know?" Camus asked. He never found out.

Supplement: Information, Decisions, and Control Procedures

The French National Assembly published an information report on the government's energy policy, which was released on October 6, 1981. The investigative commission headed by Mr. Paul Quiles started meeting on September 3, 1981 to prepare the important energy debate held at the National Assembly on October 6 and 7, 1981. The following is an excerpt from the third part of the report titled "Information, Decision and Control Procedures."

INFORMATION, SUCH AS IT HAS EXISTED UP TO NOW ON ENERGY PROBLEMS IS NOT SATISFACTORY.

Information was technocratic, did not make allowance for contradiction and had a tendency to become propaganda.

Official information on energy problems was essentially technocratic inasmuch as it was initiated for the most part, by public organizations such as E.D.F. (Electricite de France), C.E.A. (Commissariat a l'Energie Atomique), and especially inasmuch as it tended to justify the choices that were made by giving priority to the growth of these firms.

Information did not stem from a contradictory and democratic debate confronting different opinions. Such a debate never took place.

This information, all too often unilateral, was diluted in a maze of documents, the impact of which on public opinion is difficult to assess.

There is a parallel to be drawn between the way energy policy decisions were presented, and the technocratic way those decisions were made.

These objectives were singled out without any control being exercised over the responsible executive agencies and selected by the government alone and implemented by these powerful organizations without the National Assembly taking a vote to define, amongst other things, the role of nuclear energy in the global energy evaluation or how it was to be used.

This technocratic choice of energy policy objectives no longer makes it possible, in the present state of things, for the people to approve.

This is why ambitious projects involving nuclear reactors or recycling plants met with increasingly severe criticism. Indignation was even greater when it was decided to set up a nuclear plant in Plogoff.

People reacted all the more strongly against these decisions because not only did they feel they were getting no information or very little of it, but they had no means to take part in the decision-making.

Whereas a debate is the very criterion of a democratic society, it was done away with; the government's choice was presented as the only possible solution to our energy problem.

Disregarding the plurality of opinions on these energy choices, (and) failing to organize their expression, amounted to turning the information on the choices of the government into propaganda.

Because public opinion was not properly informed it was not in a position to compare the degree of risk attached to other energy sources.

Because official information minimized the dangers of nuclear energy, its opponents tended to concentrate all the dangers linked to energy policy on the nuclear (issue).

. . . we feel that it is imperative that the public be given the means to properly assess all the risks incurred by energy production in order to avoid the widening divorce between science and the population.

Up to now, information has all too often been incomplete, oversimplified or cut down.

1. Information is incomplete: presentation of the economic cost of nuclear energy is a good example of how incomplete the information is: in assessing the future cost of nuclear energy, the rising cost of recycling has not been taken into account.

A more objective presentation is necessary; the French must be able to assess accurately the global cost of nuclear kw/h (kilowatts per hour), including the cost of recycling.

2. Oversimplified or cut down information: The recycling of radioactive fuels is a good example of oversimplification; indeed, it is often indicated that recycling is a convenient, economical alternative to stocking. But recycling involves stocking. The recycling capacity of plants has been overestimated. It would be honest to present public opinion with the full range of possible choices, and to admit that the technology of recycling on an industrial scale still encounters difficulties. While hoping of course that these will be mastered, they do increasee the cost.

There still are doubts on the safety of certain techniques experimented with in labs but not on an industrial scale.

On the one hand, scientists disagree on the safety of recycling methods when it comes to radioactive nuclear fuels. On the other hand, scientists and E.D.F. and C.E.A. officials disagree on the same issue.

We received different and often contradictory answers to the following questions:

- Can one avoid recycling stocks of radioactive fuels?
- Is stocking a safer solution than recycling?
- Does the risk involved with nuclear wastes disappear in case of recycling or does it only change?
- Are we sufficiently sure to master our recycling techniques to commit ourselves to our foreign partners?

Because information holds no contradictions, alternative solutions are concealed.

Information is insufficient on two points (economic and safety) bearing on alternative solutions not chosen by the government. This lack is due to two reasons. One is institutional, the other financial.

Public organizations working in the field of energy benefit from the very powerful means of information. But their opponents do not have the financial means affording them such a large broadcasting capability. The public tends to trust a big public organization specialized in advanced technologies.

But nevertheless, with time, the various associations aiming at the defense of the environment or giving information on alternative policies have shown themselves to be serious enough for the media to accept them as acceptable sources of information.

Information is too scattered and at the same time biased and ends up lacking credibility.

As has been stressed in the Bourjol report, information on energy problems is certainly abundant but too involved in its sytle. All too often it is one sided. Either information comes from the ministries of Industry and Energy or from various agencies and commissions (all closely connected to the government), or it comes from associations who seldom get the chance to fight on equal terms. The diversity is such that energy news is often lost in the maze of general information. And because of this, people are confused as to what the real issue is.

One of the consequences is that nuclear energy information has lost its credibility. This lack of credibility is very harmful inasmuch as it leads people to distrust this source of energy.

SIX

The Nuclear Power Problem and Japan's Mass Media

Sakae Nagaoka

News Commentator, Japan Broadcasting Company (NHK)

Japan's Special Circumstances

Japan is a small, insular country whose area is only 378,000 square kilometers, of which only 30 percent is level land. Crowded into this small space are as many as 117 million people whose living standard is relatively high. Although the speed of improvement of the Japanese people's living standard has slowed down in recent years, Japan needs energy equivalent to approximately 430 million kiloliters of petroleum annually in order to maintain the present standard of living, provide jobs for the people, and maintain the current social welfare level. The Advisory Committee for Energy of the Japanese Government projects that Japan's energy needs 10 years hence will reach 700 million kiloliters in petroleum equivalent. Today, petroleum comprises 71 percent of Japan's total energy supply, coal 14 percent, hydroelectric power 5.1 percent, LNG (liquid natural gas) 4.9 percent, and nuclear power 4.1 percent.

Energy resources are extremely scarce in Japan, and the country depends almost solely on imports to meet its petroleum needs. It is very dangerous for Japan to depend on oil imports for most of its energy needs. It is self-evident that Japan needs to become less dependent on petroleum as quickly as poss-

94

ible. The type of energy to choose to replace petroleum is a constant subject of debate.

Japan has to conduct research and development with a view to utilizing whatever energy source is available, be it nuclear power, coal, natural gas, hydroelectric power, solar energy, or geothermal heat. Many Japanese today recognize that nuclear power will have to be their country's most important source of energy in the immediate future. This has been made evident by the numerous public opinion surveys conducted to date.

Japan is the only country in the world that has been A-bombed. Because of this horrifying experience, the Japanese people are far more sensitive than other peoples to the development of nuclear power and to the fear of radiation from atomic energy. The Japanese people's fear of nuclear weapons and radioactive rays has not diminished at all even 36 years after the A-bombings of Hiroshima and Nagasaki. On the contrary, their wariness of atomic energy is growing stronger and stronger these days as tensions mount in the world.

The Atomic Energy Basic Law limits the research and development of nuclear power only to its peaceful application. The law stipulates that Japan should conduct research and development of atomic energy on her own initiative and under democratic supervision, and that Japan should disclose the results and thus contribute to international cooperation. Notwithstanding, some people who are suspicious of peaceful utilization of nuclear power claim that "nuclear power generation is potentially pregnant with danger, and nuclear power generation technology is still far from perfect." They strongly demand that the development of nuclear power should be suspended immediately.

At present, 22 nuclear power plants (capable of generating 15,511 megawatts (mw)) are operating in Japan, with 11 plants (10,110 MW) under construction and six others (5,560 MW) in the stage of planning. These total 39 nuclear power plants with a combined capacity of 31,181 MW. In its long-range outlook, the Advisory Committee for Energy set the target of nuclear power generation capacity for 10 years hence at 53,000 MW. However, because the new construction and expansion of nuclear power plants is not progressing smoothly due to local residents' opposition and other reasons, the Ministry of International Trade and Industry (MITI) thinks that the original target will have to be revised downward to below 50,000 MW.

Under such circumstances and from the standpoint that it is the people who will have to decide the fate of nuclear power generation, most Japanese mass media are trying to furnish objectively data and information that will help the people make a proper judgement. Because the Japanese people are over-sensitive about nuclear power and because there are strong pros and cons as regards the peaceful application of atomic power, the Japanese mass media has to be extra careful in its treatment of the nuclear power issue so that doubts will not be cast on its unbiased and neutral attitude.

Information on Nuclear Power and Mass Media

Today, the Japanese people's biggest sources of information are newspapers and TV broadcasting. As many as 46 million copies of newspapers are published in Japan daily, which is equivalent to 2.5 Japanese, including infants, reading a newspaper everyday (according to Japan Newspaper Yearbook, 1979). One person spends an average of 20 minutes a day reading newspapers (according to a survey conducted by the Japan Broadcasting Company (NHK)).

The rate of TV diffusion in Japan is 80 percent, and one Japanese watches TV for three hours and 40 minutes daily on the average. A Japanese listens to the radio for 35 minutes on the daily average, while reading magazines and books for an average of 13 minutes daily (according to an NHK survey). A survey conducted in 1978 by the Public Relations Office, the Minister's Secretariat of the Prime Minster's Office, revealed that 74 percent of the Japanese people obtained information on the nuclear energy problem from newspapers, 67 percent from TV, 16 percent from magazines and books, and 10 percent from radio. These figures show how great an impact newspapers and TV have on the people, impressing on members of the mass media the graveness of their responsibilities.

An analysis of the media's past performance will show whether or not it was able to maintain a fair and neutral position in reporting about nuclear energy and will assess the kind of influence it had in molding public opinion as regards nuclear power generation.

The Early Stage of Nuclear Power Development

In 1963, Japan succeeded in generating nuclear power by using a research reactor and in 1966 it started nuclear power generation on a commercial basis. Even in those days, there was some opposition to nuclear power development, but most of it came from atomic energy experts. The information on nuclear energy supplied by the mass media at that time was primarily in the form of scientific commentary. The volume of information on nuclear energy was extremely limited. Moreover, because there were very few facilities in Japan, the public had little interest in nuclear power generation. Therefore, the general public was not able to obtain an adequate scientific knowledge and understanding of nuclear energy. In extreme cases, some people did not even know the difference between the atomic bomb and the mechanism of nuclear power generation. Thus, when the era of nuclear power generation arrived, quite a few people were still completely ignorant of the subject.

After 1970, nuclear power plants were constructed in close succession, and following the first oil crisis of 1973, the electric power industry and the

Japanese Government sought large-scale construction of nuclear power plants as an energy alternative to petroleum. All the power reactors installed in Japan, except the first one, are light-water reactors. These light-water reactors developed mechanical trouble one after another. Whenever a light-water reactor developed trouble in the United States (a crack in the cooling water pipe, for example), all power reactors of the same type in Japan had to be shut down immediately for inspection. If the same kind of trouble was found, the reactors had to be repaired. Because the repair of power reactors took a long time, the availability factor of power reactors dropped. There were years when the annual average availability factor of all power reactors in Japan dropped close to 40 percent.

As a natural consequence, those who opposed nuclear power generation raised their voices in the criticism, "Even a small trouble like this could develop into a major accident." But those who advocated nuclear power development insisted, "There is no danger at all because we are taking all precautions to prevent accidents." In the meantime, another group of people began to denounce nuclear power generation as economically unfeasible in view of the poor availability factor of nuclear power plants in Japan.

Apart from the pros and cons of nuclear power generation, newspaper and TV commentaries in those days called the public's attention to an entirely different angle by making the point: "The reason why Japan has to follow the United States in everything, from the repair of power reactors to their inspection for flaws, is that Japanese nuclear power technology lacks originality and initiative. Japan should establish as soon as possible its own nuclear power technology and safeguards system."

Failure of the Nuclear-Powered Ship *Mutsu*

In August 1974, the nuclear-powered ship *Mutsu* was scheduled to operate her nuclear power reactor for the first time and conduct output raising tests. However, faced with strong opposition from local fishermen against conducting the tests in her mother port in Mutsu Bay, Aomori Prefecture, the *Mutsu*, powered by a conventional engine, went out into the Pacific to conduct the output raising tests. On the fourth day after her nuclear power reactor reached criticality and the power output rose to 1.4 percent, a radiation leakage outside the power reactor was detected, followed by the sounding of an alarm. The radiation which leaked was only 0.2 mR/h, but this small leakage developed into a big issue.

Unable to continue her tests in the Pacific, the *Mutsu* intended to return to her mother port. However, because of strong opposition from local fishermen, she had to drift at sea for 50 long days. Claiming that "the authorities' explanation that the *Mutsu* was perfectly safe was a lie," local fishermen forced the government to promise to pull the *Mutsu* out of her mother port and, moreover, furnish 1,200 million yen in loans and investments to promote the local fishing industry.

The authorities, concerned with the construction of Japan's first nuclear-powered ship, and people in the nuclear power industry complained that newspapers, TV, and radio gave exaggerated reports on the accident and that some of the reports were guilty of such scientific errors as to confuse radioactive ray with radioactivity.

However, the stand taken by most of the mass media was: "No matter how small the radiation leakage, it was obviously caused by a faulty design. The problem is that a leakage occurred where it should not have. The government and those concerned with the construction of the *Mutsu* gave the impression that the nuclear-powered ship was a perfect and absolutely safe ship and are thus to blame for all the uproar over the small radiation leakage. They should have explained beforehand that the *Mutsu* would be put on a trial operation to see if it would move exactly as its designers had anticipated. Because this was not done, a small radiation leakage unnecessarily provoked a public outcry. As long as nuclear power is concerned, all matters of safety and danger alike, should be made public, and any project involving development of nuclear power should be carried out by enhancing the people's scientific understanding and on the basis of cool judgement formed by the people.

With this incident as the trigger, the government reviewed Japan's nuclear power development. As a result, the Nuclear Safety Commission was established to act as a brake on the existing Atomic Energy Commission, which, as the accelerator, had been in sole control of nuclear power development until then.

The *Mutsu* eventually was driven out of its mother port in Mutsu Bay and is now undergoing repair at Sasebo Port in Kyushu. No final decision has yet been made as to which will become her mother port to provide her with a permanent harboring place after the repair is completed. A leakage of 0.2 mR/h of radiation has precipitated an extremely unfortunate situation, with no immediate solution in sight.

From around the end of the 1970s, the Japanese nuclear power industry became gradually independent of American technology, having developed technologies of its own to a considerable extent. But just when the plant factor began to climb upward, the Three Mile Island nuclear plant accident occurred in March 1979. This news struck a hard blow to Japan's nuclear power industry. Commenting on the accident, the Japanese Nuclear Safety Commission declared that the accident was of a nature that is inconceivable in Japan's present nuclear power plant operation system. In other words, it is inconceivable in Japan to put a power reactor into operation without confirming whether or not an auxiliary pump functions correctly.

Those who opposed or were critical of nuclear power generation immediately responded that the Nuclear Safety Commission was imprudent in making this statement. They said with great emphasis, "The Three Mile

Island accident is eloquent proof that even a problem in the secondary cooling system could affect the reactor core and result in a major accident. What we had feared for a long time has finally become a reality."

Residents of localities where nuclear power plants have already been established were influenced by the Three Mile Island accident to air such views as: "Neither the nuclear power industry nor other industries can be 100 percent safe. To provide against an emergency, precautionary measures should be taken at all times so that damage from an accident could be minimized." The same thing had been repeatedly said by the mass media on every occasion.

In response to local residents' requests for precautionary measures, the Nuclear Safety Committee at long last began studying a disaster prevention system to cope with possible accidents that might happen at nuclear power plants. Local governments having nuclear power plants under their jurisdiction are now working out concrete measures to prevent disasters and cope with accidents under the guidance of the Nuclear Safety Commission.

The Tsuruga Nuclear Power Plant Accident

On the morning of April 18, 1981, the Japanese people were surprised by the news of a radiation leak at the Tsuruga Nuclear Power Plant. This news was released by MITI which called an emergency press conference at the unprecedented early morning hour of 5 a.m. Many people must have thought that a major accident comparable to that of Three Mile Island had happened in Japan.

The news was the discovery as a result of a regular inspection conducted by the Fukui Prefectural Institute of Hygienic Sciences of radioactive concentration in seaweed growing in Urasoko Bay, into which waste water from the Tsuruga Nuclear Power Plant flows. The concentration was 10 times higher than at normal times. Judging from the fact that the radioactive concentration was higher closer to the outlet of the ordinary drainage of the nuclear power plant, an accident must have occurred in the Tsuruga Nuclear Power Plant.

Subsequent investigation disclosed that a careless miss occurred in the regular process of taking out and cleaning the filter used to filtrate a minimal amount of radioactive substance contained in the cooling water of the nuclear power reactor. A worker at the plant forgot to close the valve of the water pipe leading to the tank where this filter was temporarily stored after it was taken out. Therefore, radioactive water which flooded the tank spilled onto the floor, entered the ordinary drainage outlet and flowed into Urasoko Bay.

The fact that the radioactive concentration in the seaweed growing in Urasoko Bay was 10 times higher than at normal times meant that the contamination was so small that even if a man ate 40 grams of the radioactive seaweed every day for one year, radioactive concentration in him would be only 1/25,000th of the permissible level stipulated by the International Commission on Radiological Protection (ICRP).

What made this radiation leak into a big issue was the fact that radioactive waste from the nuclear power plant flowed out from where it was not supposed to flow. In addition, although this radiation leak happened one month before it was disclosed, the Tsuruga Nuclear Power Plant did not report it either to the prefectural government concerned or to the central government.

As the investigation progressed, it was brought to light that leakage of radioactive water and cracks in the feed-water heater were detected in the same plant in the past, but no report of these accidents had been made to the proper authorities. The plant people explained that the small radioactive contamination involved was not very much different from the level of natural radioactivity and that they did not report it to the authorities because the level of contamination was below the level which obligated them to report either to the central or the prefectural government. Also, they did not want to disturb the public unnecessarily. This statement caused public criticism of the Tsuruga Nuclear Power Plant to mount.

In connection with this accident, the manner of MITI's announcement and news reporting came under fire by the Science and Technology Agency. Some people in the nuclear power industry said that MITI had made its announcement in a sensational manner and that newspapers and mass media played up the accident excessively. Although the volume of radiation leakage from the nuclear power plant was extremely small as compared with the level of radiation in the natural environment, some news reports gave the public the impression that the radioactive contamination of Urasoko Bay was so serious that fish caught in the bay could not be eaten any longer.

The public's anxiety about the attitude of such radiation experts as Tsuruga's engineers and staff, who believed they had no obligation to report a radiation leak unless it contaminated the environment seriously, and who took such leakages for granted, culminated in public criticism directed at the power plant itself.

In other words, the Japanese people, who are sensitive about radiation, wish to be kept informed always of what is happening at a nuclear power plant, and they want nuclear power plants to be operated in the open with the utmost safety precautions. Accordingly, the people think that the nuclear power plant staff, who did not report the radiation leakage on the grounds that it was below the level obligating them to report, "deliberately concealed the leakage." There was, in fact, too great a gap between the thinking of the engineers and staff of the plant who were responsible for the radiation leakage and the thinking of the public and the mass media who represent the people.

The Appropriateness of National and Local Referendums

When an atomic energy problem cannot be settled through scientific discussion, it is put to a national or local referendum in the United States and some

European countries. The Japanese people showed great interest in the national and local referendums held in the United States, Austria, Switzerland, and Sweden on issues concerning nuclear power generation. At present, however, there is no system in Japan, a parliamentary democracy, for settling controversial issues concerning nuclear power generation directly by the vote of local residents. Because nuclear power generation is a national undertaking, it is believed to be inappropriate to decide its fate by a vote of local residents. However, opinions advocating a local referendum on nuclear power issues have begun to appear in Japan.

In the case of Kubokawa Town in Kochi Prefecture, Shikoku, the mayor was in favor of allowing the construction of a nuclear power plant in the town. The town's people were equally divided for and against. A town assemblyman moved that the building of a nuclear power plant in the town be put to vote by local residents, but the motion was rejected by the assembly. Then, those residents who were opposed to the plant launched a movement to recall the mayor. The recall movement was successful, and the mayor was removed from office. This seemed to put an end to Kubokawa's nuclear power plant issue. However, when the post-recall mayoralty election was held, the recalled mayor was re-elected. During the election campaign, the mayor pledged that he would hold a referendum on the nuclear power plant issue.

A vote has never before been taken in Japan on the siting of a nuclear power plant, and it will be very interesting to see how such a vote will actually be taken. However, should it be decided to put the nuclear power issue to a vote of the townspeople, I think that a heated debate will unfold as to the appropriateness of deciding the issue in such a manner before the vote is taken.

At least half of the Japanese population is in favor of nuclear power generation, according to a recent public opinion survey, as I mentioned at the outset. But asked if they feel any apprehension about nuclear power generation, more than 50 percent surveyed replied in the affirmative. To the question, "Are you in favor of a nuclear power plant being constructed in the place where you live?," 40 to 50 percent of the surveyed replied, "No."

If, because a national referendum is out of the question, a local referendum were taken, would this not amount to seeking a decision on a particular issue where the people as a whole are in favor of its generalities but opposed to its particulars? The mass media in Japan have not yet taken up the issue of the relationship between the national energy policy (generalities) and individual nuclear power generation projects (particulars). A debate over the fine points of this relationship is expected in the future.

The Mass Media's Explanation of Its Position

In retrospect, the Japanese mass media, except for some of its members, did not necessarily oppose nuclear power development. The Japan Atomic Energy Relations Organization recently conducted a questionnaire survey of

1,000 nuclear power specialists. As much as 94 percent of those polled agreed with the statement: "It is desirable that mass media's articles and commentaries on problems concerning nuclear power generation should be written on the basis of scientific knowledge and objective facts." A high percentage of those surveyed agreed, probably because past Japanese press reports on nuclear power contained errors which could not be overlooked by experts or because the exaggerated way in which such reports were written attracted attention although they were not erroneous.

To be sure, some of the media reports on nuclear power generation probably were not completely free of scientific errors. At times, reports severely criticized the "establishment" and business. These critical reports may well be taken as the mass media's warning to them that they will be unable to obtain the public support for nuclear power development if the state's safety controls and the industry's maintenance of safeguards are insufficient. It is necessary for the mass media to examine whether their past approach was correct and whether it is possible to continue with such an approach.

Future Problems of Nuclear Power Generation in Japan

Japan's uranium resources are scarce and the country has to utilize uranium-238 to the maximum. In order to do this, Japan has to build up her reprocessing capability, treat and dispose of radioactive waste in a safe way, and put plutonium to peaceful application. In this manner, Japan has to complete its domestic nuclear fuel cycle.

Former President Jimmy Carter tightened America's nuclear nonproliferation policy towards the world. At the same time, he imposed strict restraints on the reprocessing of spent nuclear fuel at the Japanese reprocessing plant. Japan had to abide by Carter's order because of the Japan-U.S. atomic energy agreement. As a result of subsequent negotiations between the two countries, the restraints imposed by Carter were eased to some extent. The restraints are expected to be eased further under the Reagan Administration. Under such circumstances, Japan's nuclear fuel cycle is going to be completed before long. However, a number of problems might crop up when the Japanese nuclear fuel cycle is closed. They are:

1. *Prevention of the Use of Plutonium for Military Purposes*: As I stated earlier, Japan has been engaged in the development of nuclear energy to be utilized only for peaceful purposes. When the nuclear fuel cycle is completed in the future and plutonium is produced, Japan will have to establish the technology and system to completely prevent it from being used for military purposes. Thus, Japan's responsibility has become heavier.
2. *Treatment and Disposal of Radioactive Waste*: The question of how to treat and dispose of radioactive waste, which is presently piling up at a fast rate, is likely to become a weapon for those who are opposed to nuclear power

generation. Japan plans to dump low-level radioactive waste into the Pacific, in accordance with the provisions of the international convention concerned. This plan, however, has aroused opposition not only from countries in the South Pacific but also from within Japan. Should the reprocessing of spent nuclear fuel go into full operation, the volume of high-level radioactive waste will increase accordingly. This is a particularly serious problem because of its relationship to the following problem.

3. *Treatment and Disposal of Decommissioned Reactors*: A number of reactors will run their course and be decommissioned in the 1990s. The Atomic Energy Commission is now studying how to dispose of these reactors. In Japan whose land space is limited and where it is difficult to acquire sites for nuclear power plants, it is best to dismantle and remove the decommissioned reactors and construct new power reactors at the same site. However, how to treat and dispose of the huge volume of radioactive waste created as a result of the dismantling will give rise to a serious controversy in the future. Moreover, the level of radiation below which radioactive waste could be regarded as general waste will also become a subject of heated discussions.

4. *Economic Feasibility of Nuclear Power Generation*: Debates took place in the past as regards the economic feasibility of nuclear power generation. Those who were against nuclear power generation claimed that because a huge volume of petroleum is required in mining and processing uranium and in constructing power reactors and plants, nuclear power generation contributes little to an economy based on petroleum consumption and is economically unfeasible. On the other hand, those who were in favor of nuclear power generation retorted that nuclear power creates more energy than the petroleum it consumes and is economically feasible. They insisted that the only energy alternative to petroleum which is immediately available is nuclear energy. Thus, the contentions of the two opposing groups ran parallel to each other.

However, the economic feasibility of nuclear power will be debated heatedly again when it becomes necessary to ensure perfect safety in the dismantling of decommissioned reactors and in the treatment, disposal, and control of radioactive waste. I, as a member of the mass media, keenly feel the grave responsibility of the mass media when I think of its mission and capability to present to the public objectively and with scientific accuracy these controversial problems without being drawn into political and social movements.

SEVEN

Nuclear Energy Coverage: A Discussion

Nelson Smith
Leonard J. Theberge

On the evening of October 30, 1938, the Mercury Theater, under the direction of Orson Welles, broadcast a dramatization of H.G. Wells' *War of the Worlds* live over the Columbia radio network. It was a startling piece of entertainment, replete with descriptions of Martians landing in cylindrical ships in the fields of New Jersey, and the excitement was heightened by the "live, on-the-scene" news report style in which the story was told.

In fact, the drama was so urgent and compelling that it caused widespread panic—with thousands around the country actually believing the Martians had landed. One woman described her terror in this way: "I ran out of the house. I guess I didn't know what I was doing. I stood on the corner waiting for a bus and thought every car that came along was a bus and I ran out to get it." Another gave this description: " . . . What I did was just set by one window, prayin', listenin' and scared stiff, and my husband by the other snifflin' and lookin' out to see if people were runnin'."[1]

In our sophisticated media age, it seems impossible that such a panic could have occurred. After all, the show was announced as a work of fiction, carried commercial breaks, and was only one among a variety of radio shows broadcast that night. All a listener had to do was flip over to NBC, where there were no Martians being reported, to know that the Welles' program was a just humdinger of storytelling. In his 1940 book, *Invasion from Mars*, Hadley Cantril concluded that those who panicked lacked critical ability, a faculty he

104

associated with educational attainment. Among those of low education who did not panic, there was a degree of self-education from reading and other experiences.[2]

Forty years later, on March 28, 1979, near Middletown, Pennsylvania, an accident occurred in the cooling system of the Metropolitan Edison Company's Three Mile Island nuclear power facility. That night, all three television networks carried lengthy stories about the incident, and for the subsequent three weeks, Three Mile Island monopolized the nation's attention via both print and broadcast media. Network television devoted over six hours of evening news-time to Three Mile Island in twenty days.

The three networks were obviously staggered by the technological complexity of nuclear power, to which they had devoted a total of less than seven hours' time on evening news broadcasts in the preceding ten and one-half years.[3] Reporters rushed to the scene, vacuuming up pieces of information and relaying them to anchor desks, hunting down local people for on-camera reactions to the puzzling situation. There was little time for analysis. NBC's first-night coverage, typical of all three networks, was longer than average (5 minutes, 20 seconds); it utilized three field reports; interviewed pro-nuclear officials on the scene and balanced them with comments from a spokesman for Ralph Nader's Critical Mass energy project, an anti-nuclear group; and the broadcast carried conversations with nearby citizens of Goldsboro, Pennsylvania, including two elderly women who debated the relative merits of being scared, or not being scared, about the power plant.

A study of Three Mile Island coverage by The Media Institute concluded that NBC's debut performance failed to provide a description of nuclear plant operation; an explanation of why the malfunctioning cooling system presented a problem; any information as to what was happening at the plant to contain the accident; a perspective on the importance of Three Mile Island to area electric customers; and information on the importance of nuclear power to the nation's electric supply.

America's most trusted news personality, Walter Cronkite, employed unusually grim and portentous language in his reporting of the incident:

> It was the first step in a nuclear nightmare. As far as we know at this hour, no worse than that. (March 28)
>
> Good evening. The world has never known a day quite like today. It faced the considerable uncertainties and dangers of the worst nuclear power plant accident of the atomic age. (March 30)

Three Mile Island was a gripping, compelling drama—a "War on the Worlds" for the video age. People did not swarm into the streets upon hearing of the nuclear incident, but tension and fear were rampant. The incident made news around the world, and the sensation created by it made a deep, lasting impression. Several years after the events unfolded, it is not uncommon to hear of the "disaster" at Three Mile Island, although studies have confirmed that the only human harm resulting from the accident was due to stress, not radiation.

Of course, most people would argue that a direct comparison between Orson Welles' "War of the Worlds" and network coverage of Three Mile Island is silly. The former was fantasy; the latter, fact. The risks of radiation were not imaginary, like little green Martians. When the accident happened, the people living near the reactor had legitimate reason for concern.

However, consider Cantril's observation that the 1938 panic was associated with a "lack of critical ability," and consider the level of sophistication with which Three Mile Island was treated by media and public alike. For all that journalists and common folk knew, the TMI incident might have been another Martian invasion, as the technology and economics of nuclear power were alien phenomena.

It is beyond the scope of this chapter to comment on the merits and risks of nuclear energy. But it is appropriate to take note of the overheated environment in which that debate has and continues to take place and to ask whether a lack of critical ability *within media organizations* has contributed to the confusion and fear about nuclear power. More specifically, how are ordinary citizens to develop their critical faculties about such confusing and frightening technological subjects as nuclear power, when the very people on whom they depend for information are as unprepared as they were at TMI?

Dr. Robert L. DuPont, a psychiatrist who heads the Institute for Behavior and Health, Inc., was asked by The Media Institute to view a compilation of all the news stories on nuclear power generation presented on the three networks' news programs in the period between August 5, 1968 and April 20, 1979. His findings revealed that "fear was the motif of the entire series," and that journalists on the nuclear energy beat relied so heavily on worst-case scenarios that their attitude about the subject could be considered "phobic." DuPont did not minimize the real risks of nuclear power; rather, he was saying that TMI coverage was a story about what *could* happen instead of what *did* happen. Reporters, he said, exhibited a tendency toward "a malignant case of the what-ifs." Further, he said, news reports tended to undermine the voices of reassurance about nuclear energy by portraying government and industry figures as self-interested and therefore unreliable sources.[4]

It would be useful to learn some lessons from Three Mile Island. In the 1980s and beyond, democratic populations will be confronted again and again with technological issues as complicated as nuclear energy. When faced with policy choices about toxic wastes, pollutant standards, or munitions stockpiling, citizens will have a choice of three alternatives: become educated, opt out of the decision-making process, or make choices on the basis of inadequate information. If the third path is chosen—that is, if other issues find citizens dancing in the dark as they did on nuclear power—panic may become a chronic condition.

One can think of several examples during the past few decades when media organizations were called upon to exhibit technical expertise (usually after some long-simmering issue had finally reached a public boiling point). In their paper, "The Limits of the Press Corps in a Political/Technical Debate," Jude Wanniski and Robert L. Bartley examined the controversy over the anti-ballistic missile; the long argument between auto-makers and environmental groups over emission standards; and the "energy crisis" which had just begun to emerge as the paper was being prepared (early 1974). They found the press unsuited in many ways for the task of covering such issues, as they were rushed by deadline pressure, lacking in technical expertise, and tending to favor clashes between people rather than ideas.[5]

But in no single instance were the strengths and weaknesses of the press so amply demonstrated as in the Three Mile Island incident. By March of 1979, nuclear power had grown to 12.6 percent of U.S. electrical supply.[6] However, even with the barrage of energy news buffeting consumers, most people had only a dim awareness of the role of nuclear power. The Media Institute's study found that nuclear power coverage amounted to 26/100 of one percent of available evening news time on the three networks in the 10½ years preceding the incident. The researchers concluded:

> ... Of that minimal amount of coverage, almost none provided perspective upon which viewers could base assessments of the significance, risks or benefits of nuclear energy generation.... Even the straight news reports, which made up the largest percentage of time, mostly consisted of charges and statements answering those charges. Viewers were left to judge the merits of the case almost solely on statements from each extreme.[7]

Dr. DuPont's accompanying analysis of the same coverage agreed: "There is almost no mention of risk balancing."[8]

The leak in a cooling system at TMI touched off what one report labelled "several days of anxiety and near hysteria."[9] For those several days the press, the public, Metropolitan Edison, and the Nuclear Regulatory Commission flew by the seat of their pants. The channels of communication were mucked up by rumor and misinformation. Bureaucrats, businessmen, and journalists covered their bases while the public sat in suspense. It was no one's finest hour.

How should the press approach nuclear power? In order to find out, The Media Institute assembled a panel for its Ditchley Park conference which included spokesmen from the press, the nuclear power industry, government, and the ranks of those opposed to nuclear energy. Participants came from the United States, Japan, and Western Europe. They were asked to review the performance of the press so far in the area of nuclear energy, and to discuss the directions in which such coverage should move in relation to the political and social climates of their native countries.

The preceding two accounts, by Mr. Nagaoka and Mlles Monier and Lacoste, provide vivid reminders of the constraints imposed on the press by national institutions. The Ditchley Park conference used these papers as the basis for a discussion to provide a view of this critical issue across other cultures and disciplines. The discussions were divided into some five areas: the cultural context of nuclear power; media practices in covering the issue; treatment of risk; analysis of the Three Mile Island incident, and a discussion of the values represented in media approaches to the issue.

Cultural Context

CLAUDE G. PONCELET: One must recognize that nuclear power is the symbol of a major socio-cultural movement in certain Western societies. *And*, nuclear power is also a major symbol of devastation and fear. You have here a synergistic effect which reinforces these two symbolic aspects of nuclear power—which makes the problem of public acceptance very complicated. The media is intricately influenced by this phenomenon.

HANS MATHIAS KEPPLINGER: In West Germany, we have the most violent opposition to nuclear plants of any place in the world, and it has a very complicated history. Around 1970, there began on the extreme left an opposition to economic growth—that it's unnecessary, that people really don't want to increase their standard of living. Of course, this was opposed by the conservatives. The major parties, especially the SPD (Social Democrats), promoted nuclear energy as an enhancement to growth, but tried to exclude from public debate the problems associated with nuclear energy, and tried to build the plants without a broad discussion. This worked well enough for a while. However, out of the student movement there came a sort of fringe element which legitimated violent actions, and these groups were looking for new targets, one of which was the atomic industry. These violent, small groups got the attention of the media, especially television, and that put the topic on the political agenda. The major parties became badly divided, and then judicial problems ensued; for a while, nothing went on. At the moment, it seems to be easier to begin building plants again.

JEAN PELLERIN: What facilitated nuclear energy in France was that the actual problem about energy was well-known, and this helped the government to treat the problem earnestly. We import 99 percent of our oil, and we have no other large resource of energy. But there are other special factors: France, for example, is a country having one of the lowest consumptions of electricity in Europe, but this consumption keeps increasing, slowly but regularly, which is not the situation with the other countries. Another fact is that nuclear development was pushed so strongly that the nuclear industry in France is now a very important economic factor. The number of people employed in the nuclear industry and research is, depending on whether you calculate indirect employment or not, between 150,000 and 400,000 people, which is a lot in a small country. So when the price of heating oil to the consumer multiplied by twelve between 1973 and now, this stressed the importance of atomic energy.

ADRIAN HAMILTON: I think most people can understand oil issues if they get interested. Nuclear presents a different problem. In Britain, we've had a longer debate than most, but originally it was purely a financial question, or a social question, as to whether it should replace coal, and that was the whole area of the debate. Then it came up largely as a safety question, and you have to look at the circumstances and timing in which it did—along with the questions and concern about all sorts of things like chemicals and fertilizers. It's a growing concern that technology is out of hand. This is a debate in which the average member of the public, and most journalists—indeed, most *scientists* that I know—have found themselves singularly unfitted for actually making decisions about who is right and wrong, and so inevitably the press will just give two alternative views on the basis that the best way to present an argument is to give both sides.

SIR JOHN HILL: The anti-nuclear movement seems to have started in the U.S. about two years earlier than in Europe or Japan, and the arguments used were really imported into Europe as an exact analogy of what had been happening in the U.S. a year or two earlier.

ULRICH DAUNERT: I wonder if it's necessary to draw a picture which is misleading, telling people that nuclear power is the same as centralization of political or commercial power—there's a different way to look at the problem. Figures relating to West Germany show we have roughly 50 percent of electricity supplied by coal-fired power stations; roughly 20 percent of gas-fired stations for electrification; the amount of nuclear is now up to 12 percent; and for hydro, the potential is a maximum 8 percent. Gas prices have a tendency to go as high as oil prices. Which means that in our case, we have to look toward replacing 20 percent of the electricity generation coming from gas-fired power stations by other means. What can those means be? We don't have sufficient coal resources, and there's the environmental problem there anyway. So one shouldn't see the government's attitude, or the industrialists' attitude toward nuclear as if they dream of a world in which all power is supplied by nuclear energy—this would exchange one dependency for another, and no responsible government would do so. One has to look further and say, what is the margin of nuclear power which is reasonable in a specific case?

JOHN F. O'LEARY: I'd like to spend a minute sketching the history of social acceptance of nuclear power in the United States. When President Eisenhower in 1954 announced at Geneva the Atoms for Peace program, it was widely applauded as a marvel. "Turning swords into plowshares" was the theme he espoused, and that was accepted almost without criticism globally,

and certainly in the United States. We began then the evolution of the industry with very strong political backing—the Joint Committee on Atomic
Energy, the Atomic Energy Commission, and the industry counterpart, the
Atomic Industrial Forum, were a partnership that moved along the first commercial order for a nuclear plant in 1963. There was no particular public opposition to nuclear power until about the time of the Viet Nam war, when
there began to be a questioning of nuclear power in the context of bigness and
in the context of growth, and then under the National Environment Policy Act
in 1971, under the context of its environmental impact. We began by 1972 or
thereabouts to go from almost universal acceptance in the scientific community to the beginnings of rejection of nuclear power on the grounds of safety. Up until that time the Atomic Energy Commission had been regarded as
authoritative, and people believed it when the AEC said nuclear power was
safe—but particularly after 1973, when the AEC blinked on a safety matter
having to do with an accidental loss of coolant, there began to be a serious
questioning on the part of the scientific community. In the meantime, out of
the Viet Nam experience, there grew a cadre of people who were in opposition
to a lot of things government stood for. Since government stood for nuclear
power, and it in turn stood for high-technology growth and separation of
decision-making from the people, you began to find a lot of people ready to go
against nuclear power.

That ended in something quite different from the oil situation—the
development and flowering, in the mid-1970s, of a fairly organized cadre of
people who went to work for newspapers, not as journalists but as anti-
nuclear people; in the House and Senate staffs, (people) who went to work
with a mission to dispose of nuclear power; and in the Executive Branch,
where we found them turning up at EPA and CEA. It was a generational
thing, and it was done from the highest motives—this group of people
thought nuclear power was *immoral*—but out of this, there began to be the
beginnings of a coalition that by 1974 or 1975 had put the future of nuclear
power very much in joepardy, even before TMI. I suspect that we got to a
point by 1977—again, well before TMI—where the costs had become
substantially increased because of the attentuation of the construction process. We've now gotten to a point, reinforced by the Three Mile Island accident, where no privately-owned, investor-owned utility would buy a nuclear
power plant. The risk is too open-ended. From the standpoint of public
decision making, we have decided at the congressional, executive and
judicial level—and certainly at the commission level—that we don't want
anything more to do with nuclear power.

The media have played a role; I don't think it's been decisive. In this case,
I think a generation came along that looked at it, and with all its complexities, didn't like it.

NORMAN MACRAE: It seems to me that in America, the thing that holds up
the nuclear program is all sorts of extraordinary delaying court cases all

around the country. This goes back to the fact that in Great Britain, so many of our decisions are made by the civil service or by a (government) minister, whereas in America in this field so much is done by the process of law. I think the law's delays in America are appalling.

HERBERT SCHMERTZ: I think it's important to point out that nuclear power has become a very big partisan issue in the U.S. The 1980 Democratic and Republican platforms are good examples. The Democrats called for a moratorium on the building of any further nuclear power plants. The Republicans called for more nuclear power. Among those Democrats who were for the moratorium, it was part of a much bigger picture—and the press has never covered this issue. Basically, they're against the development of any but a small amount of additional domestic energy. They've opted for the conservation solution to the whole problem—and they intend to make it work by putting roadblocks in the way of U.S. energy development. Republicans opted for the supply solution, urging more production of all forms of energy including nuclear. The press has ignored the partisan, philosophical debate between Democrats and Republicans on conservation versus supply. With these people, the safety issue is not material.

Media Practices

ALAN REYNOLDS: Let me review some of the defenses offered for media performance on oil, to see if they have any relevance for nuclear. First, correct information simply didn't exist; there were no experts to be found. The industry didn't know the answers and was too secretive, and the government didn't have any answers either. Second, we shouldn't expect reporters to anticipate the future. If we lower our expectations enough, they did a good job. Third, some of the media just reflect public stupidity, rather than contributing to it. And fourth, it doesn't really matter what's reported because people don't believe it anyway. I just throw those out, because if those excuses are good enough for oil, they're good enough for uranium, too.

SIR JOHN HILL: The problem I would have in nuclear coverage is when we get what I would call "cowboy" producers—people who have come in for the first time to produce a program and are not very well informed about nuclear matters. They don't usually do it a second time—they disappear off the scene. We've complained, we've made our representation but then it's another person in three month's time.... There's really quite a distinction between those who are writing regularly, and are knowledgeable and fair, and those who come in and do a single very dramatic program which can be seriously damaging.

FRANÇOISE MONIER: What happened during the French parliamentary debate on nuclear power was very interesting, very productive. The reporters covering the debate were essentially the same as always, but the coverage was so good, so complete—giving very specific economic insights, treating the risk problem in a very fair way. One of the explanations an editor gave is that there wasn't a very strong government line before the debate, and so the editors let journalists question everyone—then gave it a lot of space, because the debate was so open. The methods of coverage were very special with *teams* of journalists covering the debate, political reporters, science correspondents, economists, all doing columns. The question is, will it last—or was it only a special event?

MICHEL ANFROL: Yes, for the first time we sent two different teams to cover that debate—our science and energy editors, and the political correspondents.... I must say, though, that the C.A., the French communicatory commission, is a kind of "public service." We have three networks and all three are part of the same monopoly. And in all candor, there has been some pressure from the government in the past ten or twelve years to support our nuclear program, since we're all part of the "public service." So we were, perhaps, a little bit biased in favor of the program—we were told, after all, that as good citizens, since we needed to import 99 percent of our energy, we'd rather back our national program than go against it.

JEAN PELLERIN: But it is so difficult to catch the attention of the public. As a part of the information campaign about energy suggested by the government just before the parliamentary debate, one of the networks put on a two and one-half hour debate during prime audience time, near 8:00 in the evening. On the other French networks were two movies—one with Romy Schneider and one a police movie. What was the percentage of people watching the three programs? For Romy Schneider, 47 percent; for the police film, 47 percent; and for the very important national debate, 6 percent.

WILLIAM D. SMITH: And I guarantee that of that 6 percent, 5½ percent had already decided what side of the issue they were on anyway. They were watching it to reconfirm what they already believed.

JEAN PELLERIN: My impression is that people coming back from work in the evening want entertainment, not to go to school and learn a difficult and technical issue.

Issues of Risk

ROBERT L. DUPONT: In looking at the media coverage of the danger of nuclear power, I find three issues that are problems, all having general applicability for other technologies. First is "who controls the risk?" If the risk to health is controlled by someone else, it is exaggerated in the public mind. If the risk is controlled, or perceived to be controlled, by one's self then it is minimized. Much of the opposition to nuclear power hangs its hat on this issue—the whole question of nuclear power being "anti-democratic" really gets back to who controls the risk rather than to how large or small the risk is. The second issue is whether the risk shows up in one big event or a in a lot of little events. Prototypes for serious risks spread over time and space are deaths associated with cigarette smoking and automobile accidents. These risks are minimized while risks from one big event, like a plane crash, are exaggerated. The media play a significant role in exaggerating concentrated risks and minimizing distributed risks. A third issue is whether the risk is unfamiliar or familiar. If it is unfamiliar, it tends to be exaggerated. Modern phobia treatment is based on the need to get the person into the fear-producing situation repeatedly so that it becomes familiar and therefore less fear-producing.

Energy, since 1973, has become a sort of inkblot test to play out our collective psychological life. The media play a central role in this process—in one sense the media reflect the distortions and, in another sense, the media create and sustain them. There is a major unmet responsibility for the media to help separate issues of health risk from issues of fear. We need to find ways to get past the fear issue and into the health risks of nuclear power compared to alternate means of producing electricity so the public can see how the real risks of nuclear power compare to other, more familiar, risks. At this point, the public debate about nuclear power is being obscured by fear. This fear, as it is reflected in the media, is itself exaggerated by these three easily understandable but unconscious psychological processes. By contract the media could play a positive role by separating fear from health risks. The media could also help by putting the health risks into perspective not on the basis of what could happen but has happened during the more than 20 years nuclear power has been used commercially.

TOM BURKE: People talk about risks and benefits as though benefits were also facts, which they are not. Whether you see the production of more electricity as a benefit or not depends on where you see electricity fitting into the overall energy policy. There's been an attempt to create a sort of risk/benefit calculus, which seems to me illogical at best—and this is where the media have the most trouble presenting the character and real issue of the debate.

CLAUDE G. PONCELET: I agree with Mr. Burke about the risk/benefit analysis. Risk is more of a relative aspect, and the risk/benefit situation is what energy policy is based on—that's where the public really needs to be informed, the relative risk of generating electricity with nuclear power or coal.

HERBERT SCHMERTZ: I'm encouraged by the reports from France and Japan, two countries that were 90 percent or more dependent on foreign sources. They made a judgment that from the political and economic standpoint the risks of *not* going to nuclear were substantially worse than any of the hypothetical risks of the worst cases developed by scientists. I suggest that the day the U.S. recognizes the risks of not having enough energy, the public will run absolutely roughshod over the Jane Fondas of this world and will demand nuclear energy.

ALAN REYNOLDS: The U.S. has options France and Japan do not have. I expect that if we decontrolled natural gas, that alone might suffice to fill the gap until nuclear power; when you have such a dependence on outside sources as these countries have, you might well choose nuclear even though it were more costly than oil or coal, and that would be a rational social decision. It seems to me that on risk reporting, the lack of perspective is a critical one. There is very little recognition that all forms of energy entail risk—some of them are not small, like an LNG tanker exploding, or a dam breaking and flooding. Coal is obviously dangerous to mine; many people die from it; it pollutes the air. Natural gas doesn't pollute, but there are gas leaks. We tried burning garbage in New York, and found that it spreads disease. There are no 100 percent safe options except to go back to grubbing a living with your bare hands out of the soil. Even conservation—which sounds totally safe—well, some people have been found to overinsulate their homes and suffocate.

TOM BURKE: I have a feeling that in the U.S. and to some extent here, the nuclear industry brought a lot of the problems it now has with credibility down on its own head by not trusting the public to make some reasonably good judgments about what risk it could and could not live with . . . . The feeling was clear for a long time that the industry, particularly in the U.S., would not come clean about what its real problems were—not insurmountable, not that they couldn't be overcome, but they kept saying, there's nothing here for anyone to worry about.

ADRIAN HAMILTON: That's right; one of the problems, it seems to me, about nuclear power and a great many of the technological subjects, is that people are reacting—particularly journalists—almost because they believed too much originally, and that companies and scientific communities have set up too high ideals and (have) not adjusted people to the fact of continual risk. We've been brought up, most of us, to believe that it's somehow risk-free. And therefore as soon as you get a small incident, it ruins the credibility altogether.

Three Mile Island

ROBERT S. GORALSKI: We don't have experts covering stories. It's the White House reporter, the congressional reporter. One day he's an expert on labor disputes, the next day on airline safety, the next day on aid to Africa . . . . I saved some bulletins coming out that Friday morning at Three Mile Island. One said one-quarter of the core had melted, "according to a congressional aide." That was killed 45 minutes later. But another, an hour and a half later, said Governor Thornburgh was considering evacuating 6 counties around TMI. Somebody asked why he hadn't done it immediately, and the Governor's aide explained: "because he doesn't know if it's necessary." A professional on the wire would never have permitted those [bulletins] to go out. It was a Harrisburg man covering state politics, who suddenly was covering a very important story.

JEFF GREENFIELD: The communications consultant to the Kemeny Commission said that the sources of information at TMI were far more to blame than the press, because when you combine the lack of information with the wrong information and the confusion of the commissioners . . . . The reporters on the scene were not doing a history of nuclear power in America, but were trying to answer a fairly basic question — what was the *danger* after the authorities had announced the possibility of a meltdown? The press was being given very bad information, and when the country asked a perfectly legitimate question, "Was this thing going to melt down?," of course they produced a kind of reporting that emphasized the great danger.

ROGER PETERSON: I commend you to look at the minutes of the meeting of the NCR (Nuclear Regulatory Commission) on March 29, 1979, and look at the confusion going on in the organization that was supposed to be in charge of protecting everyone and knowing all about this. That's one of the most frightening things I've ever read.

LEONARD J. THEBERGE: The Kemeny Commission put blame all around; there was no one institution, government, industry, or press which came out looking terribly well. We did a study based on specific recommendations of the Kemeny Commission on how information should be handled in a future nuclear crisis. They recommended that the industry take certain steps to improve its public information capabilities, that states with nuclear facilities do the same, and that the media have people available and experienced to report on accidents. We sent a questionnaire to government, utilities, and major news organizations — print, radio and the networks. We received a good response in general, about a 75 percent reply rate. Utilities took the Kemeny recommendations very seriously; state governments also did; so did the print media. But the broadcast media had done little or nothing to prepare itself for future accidents. The networks didn't respond to the questionnaire or phone calls we made.

Media Values

ANTHONY J. PARISI: My observation is that unlike European vs. American coverage of oil, coverage of nuclear energy has been bad on both sides of the Atlantic, and both in terms of anti-and pro-nuke reporting. The anti-nuclear reporting is laced with tremendous numbers of scientific inaccuracies — great scare stuff, exaggerations, improbable outcomes, and that sort of thing. The pro-nuclear reporting accepts without question that nuclear is absolutely necessary. I think the big story of nuclear, the starting point, is essentially an economic one, not a safety or environmental one. Before society must answer the question "is this form of energy safe?," it must first decide whether it's necessary. In the U.S. — where, granted, it's a lot easier to wage a campaign against nuclear on economic grounds than in Europe — if you look at the numbers, you find it very difficult to find nuclear competitive. The problem with nuclear is that the only way to use it is to convert it into electricity — and the problem with that is that electricity costs a lot more than other forms of energy delivered to the consumer.

BEATRICE LACOSTE: I agree with you that nuclear reporting has been bad — the question is, should there *be* pro- and anti-nuclear reporting? It should be more purely informative.

ANTHONY J. PARISI: No question; but to me, the most informative stories will come out of an analysis of nuclear on its economic merits. And I very rarely see that done.

SIR JOHN HILL: I think you've got to recognize the difference between rational debate with a reporter who is trying to find out the truth and the whole truth, and someone who is only using a big industry like the nuclear industry as a suitable vehicle for putting his general views across. For example, there are many people on television who are "for the little man," sorry for the widow living in the cottage, against the big oil company or nuclear authority. And I've seen on British television an anti-nuclear program put on by a particular researcher and producer, and sometime later, remember seeing by chance another program about a natural gas terminal being built somewhere in Scotland. The argument against the natural gas terminal was exactly the same as the argument against the nuclear power station. There was the sympathetic interview with the old lady sitting in her cottage, who had lived there for 50 years, and yes, she was terribly frightened that she would be blown up by this wicked terminal, followed by a very aggressive interview with what turned out to be an American oil man, who knew everything about it but was stopped in his tracks by the agressive approach of the interviewer. Now, at the end of the latter program, I saw it was the same producer — but I had already identified him by his technique. These are the programs I find difficult. There wasn't any dialogue with us, nor, I'm sure, with the oil company; it was simply someone putting the producer's point of view across.

TOM BURKE: In the matter of economic versus safety analysis, I don't think we're anywhere near in a position where the media are presenting clearly what the issues are. I also have a big question in my mind as to whether that matters — whether what the media have to say about this issue is engaging at any point in the policy-making process. The area where it's been most difficult is this question of science and value, and the difference between facts and values. I have a feeling the media accept very uncritically what is stated as a fact—not only by the official bodies, but by the "anti" bodies as well. For example, the sort of constant statement that "nuclear is cheaper than coal" is accepted as a fact, when it's not a fact; it's a judgment, one which is extraordinarily questionable.

CLAUDE G. PONCELET: While agreeing with Mr. Parisi's point, I must also say that the economic conditions around nuclear power have been very much influenced by the treatment of risk in the media—there's a link that can't be ignored. The media have tended to treat any nuclear event, by definition, as a controversial event. We see coverage of news related to risk that should never be news. But another factor is the skepticism the media have come to display in listening to experts in this field. It's not unusual to see a statement by the National Academy of Science given equal weight with a single scientist working for an anti-nuclear group—a complete lack of recognition as to where the consensus stands. The public then concludes that there is a scientific controversy on the subject. It's also led to the unusual situation that it's almost impossible for the public to have an objective expert presenting information because almost by definition, any time an objective scientist makes a statement, he is immediately defined as "pro-industry" . . . and the same is true on the anti-nuclear side. So it's very difficult to pass on information, and it's a vicious circle.

TOM BURKE: I'm still looking for this mythical beast called the "objective scientist." I've not run across him, particularly in this area, any more than I've run across the "objective journalist"—he simply doesn't exist. One thing that's happened, a very important part of the transformation of the debate on nuclear power, is that monopoly on information held by those people directly concerned with nuclear energy has been broken by those people of the younger generation to whom Mr. O'Leary referred earlier. That's changed the situation. There's no such animal as an objective scientist who's going to give "the facts" to the media. It seems that one thing Watergate taught us was that the coverup is infinitely more interesting than the actual story.

JEFF GREENFIELD: If you assume—pardon me, philosophy teachers—that there is an objective reality about, say, economics, or about whether nuclear power is safe, then you're not asking the questions most people want answered. You're not asking "Are you fair?," "Do you have an axe to grind?"

ADRIAN HAMILTON: One of the problems here is that western society, in particular, has progressed through the idea of a free debate between opposites. The feeling that's been there since Greek philosophy and through the Renaissance, which is profoundly imbued in the whole of our culture, has not been one of consensus, but of debate—and the belief that the individual and his idea, the minority view, is the great contribution toward progress. One of the questions we have to ask ourselves about the present situation is that, for the broad masses of the public, the scientific consensus was perfectly acceptable for a long time. People said, "Well, if the government says all these chemicals are safe, and there's an approval procedure for drugs, then these must be all right." That has broken down, particularly in the press. I notice among my colleagues an instinctive reluctance any longer to believe in anybody, advisory or otherwise, who believe they're right.

TOM BURKE: There's no shortage of experts; there's a shortage of authority. And that is the real problem for the media. Especially when you have generalized journalists who actually go to different experts and get completely different testimony, and have no basis on which to resolve the conflict, and basically, therefore, only report their own prejudices. That's not a critical statement; I don't think people have much choice. And now there's been this quite conscious effort on the part of people outside the industry to actually acquire expertise and authority, and that creates a very much more complicated situation.

CLAUDE G. PONCELET: I would disagree with Mr. Burke there. I do believe that if it is indeed difficult to find objective scientists, it is, however, possible to find a scientific consensus. I would advance, for an example, the controversy over low-level radiation, where the bulk of the large scientific and medical associations have very carefully and categorically expressed themselves that low-level radiation essentially presents no risks. On the other hand, I also believe that the scientific community of which I am part, and the industry generally, has to bear a large part of the blame in that scientists and industrial scientists have been notably ineffective in communicating these ideas through the media. This has to do with the way scientists are trained to communicate to one another. It's a matter of ethics for a scientist to equivocate. If there's the slightest possibility that something wrong could happen, you always concede it out of ethical consideration. If, however, you do that with the general public or politicians, I think you may be misleading the public or the politician.

ANTHONY J. PARISI: Maybe we need as an integral part of the system some kind of advisory body on such heady questions as the science of nuclear energy. In the United States, there is an organization called the Scientists' Institute for Public Information, which tries to line up scientists on both sides of any scientific question, and then provide these names and encourage them to be available to reporters. I wonder if that would be helpful elsewhere.

BEATRICE LACOSTE: It might be in France, because there, one of the problems is finding a scientific source. Very often they are not willing to talk to the press, either because they are afraid of being misquoted, or because they don't feel free to. Of course, another problem is that a journalist should tend to challenge what a scientist will tell him, but may not feel confident to do so—yet should he just accept everything he's told by a scientist, and give it back to the public?

SAKAE NAGAOKA: It is quite difficult to get consensus among scientists, because there is no 100 percent certainty among scientists. So scientific discussion or argument could go on forever. That is where we need political and social settlement. But even in this case, we have to provide the public with accurate scientific information, simple and unbiased, in order for them to make the correct political and social decisions.

Notes

1. Robert E. Lane and David O. Sears, *Public Opinion* (Englewood, N. J.: Prentice-Hall, Inc., 1964) p. 79.
2. *Ibid.*, p. 80.
3. Reported in *Television News Covers Nuclear Energy: A Ten Year Perspective*, The Media Institute, Washington, DC. 1979.
4. Robert L. DuPont, *Nuclear Phobia—Phobic Thinking About Nuclear Power* (The Media Institute, Washington, DC. 1980).
5. Jude Wanniski and Robert L. Bartley, "The Limits of the Press Corps in a Political/Technical Debate" (Paper presented at the Conference on Expert Advice and Democratic Choice, convened by the Center for Policy Study, University of Chicago, at Wingspread, Racine, Wisconsin, April 4-6, 1974).
6. The Media Insitute, *Television News Covers Nuclear Energy, Op. Cit.*, p. 13.
7. *Ibid.*, p. 53.
8. DuPont, *Nuclear Phobia.*, p. 6.
9. Jon G. Udell, and Roberta Hornig, "Resources, Energy and The Environment," *Reporting on Business and the Economy*, ed. Louis M. Kohlmeier, Jr. et al. (The Foundation for Economic Freedom, Washington, DC. 1981), p. 133.

PART THREE

Institutions

EIGHT

British Media and Energy Policy

Norman Macrae

Deputy Editor, The Economist

Journalists are bad at assessing their own trade. I have worked for the past 30 years on a "viewspaper," not a newspaper, so many colleagues will disagree with some part of what I say. But it is pleasant to write on one of the few media subjects where British (indeed, European) systems work better than American ones.

On a limited number of minimally complicated microeconomic matters, including energy policy, the British process of decision-influencing, decision-taking, and decision-execution is more sophisticated than the American one. Media comment on them is accordingly more intelligently targeted and sometimes better informed.

This may seem an opinionated statement, equivalent merely to saying that my own (probably right-of-centre) views on oil policy are more frequently expressed in the British press and broadcasting than they are in the American press and broadcasting. I honestly do not think that the difference here is one of right-left divide. As a "viewspaperman" who has visited America in most of the years since 1949, I was surprised at the relative lack of sophisticated media comment on American energy policy in the period 1950–70 when American oil policy was extraordinarily favourable to the domestic oil industry, and in the period after 1973 when American oil policy was extraordinarily antagonistic to the domestic oil industry. Simultaneously, as would certainly have been argued insistently in British "heavy newspaper" comment

123

and British televised documentaries; international and domestic events were making it desirable to switch policy precisely the other way round.

In the microeconomics of the oil industry, the dominating fact during the 1950s and 1960s was that oil sucked up out of deserts (virtually, just by turning on a tap) arrived at only a fraction of the cost of oil extracted from much more expensive land in Texas by the more costly processes of tertiary recovery. The sensible microeconomic policy then was to get oil from the cheapest source. Instead, American policy in this period was geared to making a few Texans and Californians into millionaires by protecting the domestic oil industry and by giving these Texans and Californians depletion allowances and other tax breaks. As a result they depleted America's oil as fast as possible during a period when pumping it up was least economic.

It was said to be important for reasons of national defense that the United States "keep a domestic oil industry in being." As oil is a depletable resource, the real argument based on national defense was clearly the opposite. For the day when foreign oil supplies became unreliable (a day that was always likely to come) it would be desirable to have as much American oil in the ground as possible. Few in the American media pointed this out during this period, and visiting foreign newsmen (who were pointing it out) often asked why.

The wrong explanation we were given at that time was the "political power of the oilmen in America." It was said that fabulously rich oil millionaires had a stranglehold on local television stations and politicians, often through direct ownership. Had this argument been true, there would have been one comfort in it. When the day arrived when foreign oil supplies became cartelised, American press comment would presumably be wholly in favour of encouraging domestic production even more energetically—thus breaking the cartel by quickly creating a glut.

Precisely the opposite occurred. When in late 1973, OPEC raised its asking price for oil to way above the equilibrium level, the old American oil policy became suddenly sensible. It was therefore instantly reversed. The three desirable microeconomic policies after the OPEC price hike in 1973 were:

1. Encourage domestic oil production in America by making it very profitable. Instead, policy in America switched to price controls and windfall profit taxes.
2. Discourage consumption of oil products by making them much more expensive. Gasoline prices had always been lower in the United States than in Britain, chiefly because such very low American gasoline taxes were imposed. The usual explanation before 1970 was that "gasoline is largely a home-produced commodity in the United States, and taxes are higher in Europe in order to keep an imported product out." Yet from 1970 to 1979, while OPEC quadrupled its price for crude oil, American gasoline prices rose only from 35½ cents to 88 cents a U.S. gallon, a rise of under 150 percent during a period when America was growing less self-sufficient in oil. From 1970 to

1979 gasoline prices in Britain rose from 62½ cents to $2.16 a U.S. gallon, a rise of nearly 25 percent during a period when Britain was becoming much more self-sufficient in oil. Although there was political resistance to increases in gasoline taxes in Britain, the quality newspapers generally advocated taxes on oil consumption and criticised tax rises on oil production. Quality newspapers in America often did the reverse.

3. Encourage alternative means of energy production by relaxing environmental controls that: block the building of nuclear power plants, dams, and pipelines; impede the burning and open-cast mining of coal; and make it obligatory to burn fuel in the least fuel-saving way. Instead, those environmental controls were tightened in America in the most cost-unconscious way, with the press often shrilly on the side of the extreme environmentalists and with American teachers in particular preaching shockingly mendacious calculations (like those in the Club of Rome's first "Limits to growth" booklet) to their students.

For those of my viewpoint there has been an obvious improvement in American energy policy in recent months, but it was not led on by media comment. It did owe something to articles by professors of economics and the like that appeared in the press, but newspaper reporting was not integrated with those learned and surprisingly readable pieces. Some American editors say that it is deliberate policy to keep comment on events the province of outside experts (professionally edited to make them understandable to their readers), and reporting of events the province of unbiased newsmen. I will be returning to this argument later. It is, frankly, quatsch. Respectable, crusading journalism in the fields of human rights, civil order, anti-corruption, moral investigations, environmentalism, and so on, is more common and professional in America than in Britain. But crusading or even informational journalism on a limited range of mostly microeconomic subjects is not so common in America as in Britain. The reasons for this lie deep in various features of British government practice and press structure. Some of these features have damaging consequences for other aspects of British life, but they accidentally help to make for a more informed press on microeconomic subjects.

These features can be collated (with only a little journalistic wriggling) under one or another of the five guidelines or "questions to be answered" which The Media Institute sent to those of us preparing papers on particular countries for this colloquium.

The guidelines I was asked to consider when writing about Britain were:

1. *The relationship between people and government in Britain: that is, what kind of legal and political framework exists for deciding upon and implementing public policy?* The most important point to recognize here is that permanent civil servants have a much larger role in economic policy-making in Britain than in America. Consequently, while newspapermen in Washington ask the question "Which congressmen from which districts will

fight these proposals?" newspapermen in Britain are asking "What is the view on this matter likely to be formed by the treasury knights?"

2. *The relationship between government and the media: that is, what kinds of constraints, both obvious and subtle, may the British government exercise over media organizations?* The most important points here are that Britain has more restrictive libel and contempt of court laws than has America; also broadcasting was originally set up in Britain as a monopoly, with excruciatingly boring rules (which carried on when broadcasting became more competitive) about "just balance" and "fairness" as between political parties. All of these restrictions have limited freedom of speech in Britain, but they have also had two subtle effects: first, they have made investigative reporting of alleged misdemeanours less frenetic than it became in America after Watergate, and secondly, they have made microeconomic issues (particularly ones like energy policy, without great party commitment) among the ones on which the brightest TV producers like to present informed documentaries. In a broadcast documentary asking "What to do about OPEC?" one can escape from the boring necessity of having a Tory MP, a Labour MP, and a Liberal/SDP MP to say meaningless opposite things to each other in the studio, and take up half the program's time.

3. *The media culture: what is the relative strength of each medium in Britain in delivering news and creating public opinion?* There are three national Sunday newspapers in Britain of high quality and considerable influence among thinking people (*Sunday Times*, *Sunday Telegraph*, and *The Observer*), together with half-a-dozen more populist national Sunday newspapers which sometimes try to exert influence, too. We on *The Economist* certainly regard the three "heavy" Sundays as our main competitiors among the weekly viewspapers in Britain (which is one reason why we have tried to become more international, since other, more purely national weeklies have always looked like money-losers). Among the national daily newspapers there are also four "heavies" (the *Times*, *Guardian*, *Daily Telegraph*, and the *Financial Times*), the populist national daily papers which sometimes seek political influence (and the well-written *Daily Mail* now has it), and the provincial daily newspapers. The wide spread of the "heavy" national Sunday and daily press in Britain means that the television networks do not have the same overpowering influence as in America. Indeed, the BBC and ITV networks are not supposed to impart opinions, but everybody knows the views of their main interviewers which usually range from slightly right to slightly left of centre. To this same narrow range of opinion belong most of the people working on the four heavy weeklies (the three Sundays, plus *The Economist*), those working on the four heavy dailies, and usually the "treasury knights" or "permanent secretaries" heading the civil service.

Most of the people at or near the top of the departments in the civil service received first- or top second-class honours degrees in subjects like economics, and usually at Oxford or Cambridge. Many of us writing on *The Economist* (including me) did the same. Although I do not think like a top civil servant (and top civil servants would insist even more loudly to politicians that they do not think like me), the same sorts of microeconomic ideas seem instantly crazy to all of us: for example, the sorts of ideas that dominated American energy policy in 1950-79.

The supposed political neutrality of the television networks makes this system even more incestuous. When there is an "expert" issue like a sudden new energy problem, the television and radio networks tend to call in journalists from one of the four heavy weeklies or the four heavy dailies to discuss it.

4. *The nature of British media institutions, their organization and funding. Question: How does Britain keep all those heavy newspapers profitable?* Answer: It doesn't. Although many papers, including *The Economist* are fortunately still making money, most of the others usually are not. Economic considerations suggest that the three heavy Sundays will some day (and very profitably) merge into one, and that the four heavy dailies will some day become only two. But individual press lords and rich businessmen maintain money-losing respectable newspapers either because they think this will give them political influence or kudos as public-spirited figures (actually, it doesn't), or because they see that British newspapers are run so inefficiently with such ridiculous trade-union restrictions that the introduction of any efficiency should bring most newspapers to the top of the tree and make money (which is true, but this is a game which only one newspaper in each category can win). Meanwhile the false hopes or optimism of the tycoons fortunately keep alive eight heavy newspapers, with eight economics editors who co-operate in some way with eight energy correspondents so that the level of discussion on energy policy in the British press is more sophisticated than in the American press.

5. *The impact of public opinion on the creation of policy in Britain, and vice versa.* It will be convenient to include under this heading any matters not discussed above, such as the lack of regional pressures in Britain (no snowbelt versus sunbelt, because we don't have the latter) and the disadvantage in America that financial journalists tend to congregate in New York while political correspondents are stuck in overpolitical Washington.

Each of the five subheadings will now be briefly discussed in turn.

Civil Servants Decide Policy

The senior and permanent civil service plays a much larger role in policy-making in Britain than it is conventional to admit. The top bureaucracy plays an even larger role in Japan and France. Serious journalists specializing in economic and similar areas therefore direct their writing to influence (and to be fed by) these fairly erudite top bureaucrats. There are cynical historical reasons why formerly aristocrat-ruled nations like Britain and Japan have arranged to be governed in complicated matters partly by meritocratic bureaucracies. Those reasons have been best described by an irreverent Irish-American, Senator Daniel Patrick Moynihan, when he said of Europe and Japan.

> The status of the higher civil servants there is, ostensibly, an achieved one, but the achievement came before the career began.... It lay in education and the taking of examinations: not quite a matter of birth, but something inherited from a prior period of life, a partly aristocratic principle.... American civil servants, striving from one grade to another, no sooner breaking out of the low reaches than to face sudden death by "up or out" selection boards, can never fathom...

Broadly speaking, governments in London sift their policy recommendations through civil servants, who review proposals to see if they are intellectually respectable. Administrations in Washington throw their policy recommendations at Congress, which examines them to see if they will cause political rows. Newspapermen in Washington become experts at discovering whether particular proposals are going to prove politically acceptable on the Hill. Newspapermen in London find out what is going to happen (and thus satisfy their innate urge to be ahead of events) by gauging "what will be the view on these issues of the treasury knights?"

There are three departments of state in Britain that are not ruled by the treasury knights, because they are captives of special interests. These departments are (1) the Ministry of Labour (now called the Department of Employment), which is run by the trade unions; (2) the Ministry of Agriculture, which is run by the farmers' pressure group but is not presently very important; and (3) the Ministry of Defence, which is run by the generals, admirals, and air marshals, but they are rapidly losing power. In British newspapers the labour, farming, and defence correspondents write their copy shot through with economic howlers from emotional and innumerable pressure groups—like American newspapermen writing on energy and other microeconomic subjects.

It would be wrong to suppose that the rule of the treasury has been beneficial to Britain on most of the matters on which their expertise holds sway. The treasury knights have enjoyed Keynesian fine tuning, because this has given them power and great annual job satisfaction when introducing budgets. They are always rescuing big bankrupt private or nationalized industries, partly because there will be some senior civil servant in charge of subsidizing British Steel or British Leyland, and his empire will be diminished when these absurd subsidies are at last abolished. They have tried for far too long to stick to fixed exchange rates, because this has enabled them to tell chancellors of the exchequer, "there is a grave sterling crisis and you must jump through our hoops." They brought Britain into the European Economic Community (EEC) when most voters and, probably, politicians of all parties were really opposed.

On the first three of these four controversial subjects (fine tuning, rescuing lame ducks, resistance to devaluation) my own writing has been generally critical of the treasury knights through the years. On at least one of the subjects (my belief—in the event, justified—that devaluation was inevitable

before the end of 1967), I was put in the doghouse by the British establishment, there was a brief period when treasury knights were told not to talk to
irresponsible devaluers like Macrae, and I could see why more sensitive
radicals sometimes get very cross with the secret constraints on free speech
within the system.

On the fourth of these controversial subjects (whether Britain should join
the EEC) I happened to have been in favor of joining from the time of the
founding six's preliminary conference in Messina in 1955. When the treasury
became pro-EEC—entirely because of the retirement of one civil servant,
and his replacement by another—I saw from the sunnier side what radicals
rightly call the con game: secret breakfasts where plots were laid to win important converts to the cause, memos leaked to me, parties at Downing Street
with what was called the favored journalists' "white commonwealth," and an
invitation to spend a night down at the then prime minister's country house of
Chequers.

Today I am not sure whether it was right for Britain to join the EEC,
although on balance I still support it. But the country was helped towards this
extraordinary step by contacts between civil servants and journalists, with
particular politicians joining in later, before they had told their own colleagues that they intended to do so.

This might be called the dubious side of the establishment system of
British journalism, and Americans are probably right when they are occasionally shocked by it. But there are advantages in what one can honestly call
a spontaneous combustion of sophistication on particular economic issues.
The one article you cannot sensibly write in the British press is the sort of article which says, "Here are the laws of supply and demand, let us pretend that
we can repeal them." On microeconomic matters the treasury knights maintain some educated tie with common sense. But American newspapermen,
trying to find out how congressmen from the snowbelt will vote on energy
prices, tend to suppose that congressional votes can overrule market forces.
In America, the process of laughing at economic sottises does not start early
enough.

When President Carter came down from his Maryland mountain top in
1979, he announced a policy that he thought was part of a preview to the next
year's reelection campaign. Most of the phrases in his energy sermon then
would not have been made by a politician in Britain, because they would have
been instantly roasted in the serious press as being quite absurd. The President declared: "Beginning this moment, this nation will never use more
foreign oil than we did in 1977—never." It is a nonsensical pretence that any
man in 1979 can freeze international trading patterns for all future ages. He
promised simultaneously to throw great sums of public money into discovering or developing particular synthetics that may not exist. All economic
history has shown that you can discover things quickly if you make their discovery profitable, but if you merely subsidize investment in ventures named

by politicians you will launch white elephants (a politician in Britain would have known that eight newspapers and two TV channels would be pointing out that lesson of economic history). Most absurdly, President Carter announced "as a matter of law" that utility companies should cut their use of oil by 50 percent in the next decade, and that $10 billion more should be invested in public transport. These statements represented the replacement of market economics by command economics based on figures politically created as an election stunt, and in the British press they were portrayed as such.

American policy also attempted to use command economics, instead of market economics, in distributing oil products. When the oil embargo made imports of oil into Britain temporarily short at the end of 1973, one British Ministry (over the opposition of the Treasury) issued petrol-rationing coupons as a precautionary measure. The disastrous result was that all 10 million vehicles in the country filled their tanks from half-full to full, and a real shortage at the pumps began. At that time I wrote an article, originally called "Sell your petrol coupons now," in which I argued petrol rationing could not last for even a few weeks in the proposed form. It could only work if petrol coupons were allowed to be sold by one recipient to another in a free market, so that there was some element of pricing in the rationing system. In America, this view was regarded as heretical. In Europe it would have become official policy had there been a real shortage of oil after 1973.

Of course, there was not a real shortage of oil immediately after 1973. The rise in OPEC's price drove the stuff straight into glut until the Shah of Iran went into exile. There was then, in 1979, temporary shortage again, and gas lines appeared in the United States. At that time America was still trying to allocate gasoline across the country by a control system, even at the height of the summer holiday season. Inevitably, the system brought grave shortages of petrol (and long lines at the pumps) in the areas which people lacked enough gas to drive away from, balanced by gluts at the seaside resorts where they lacked the gas to drive to. The right policy was to allow a rise in price in areas which were short of gas, yet in free enterprise America this was called illegal, and was made to look immoral by the media when it occurred. In Britain, during the brief period of some shortages then, press comment went on the opposite tack: there were complaints when some filling stations closed down on the weekends (when holiday motorists wanted them), and there was praise for those who were commercially sharp enough to open on weekends and charge a few pennies more per gallon.

Libel and Monopoly

Britain suffers from overstrict laws concerning libel and contempt of court. They make it difficult for British newspapers to reveal the activities of obvious criminals. There are several corrupt local government bodies in Britain, almost always in areas where the social mix means that one political party has been in power for decades. However, batteries of lawyers frighten newspapermen away from revelations about them. In business, much incompetence and some malfeasance proceed unreported upon, although the self-regulatory systems within the City of London probably do stop criminal malfeasance in protected businesses from proceeding for long. Probably, indeed, these systems impose a "gentlemen's ethic" too snobbishly.

The use of the honors system (knighthoods, and the like) also keeps a gentlemen's ethic in being, which is why there was such a fuss when Prime Minister Harold Wilson used the system to ennoble friends or financial contributors to his political campaigns who did not pass all of the establishment's tests for gentlemen. This complicated system means that the self-cleansing or examination procedure is carried out rather surreptitiously within British society, without screaming newspaper headlines or scoops that are *succés de scandale*. A very major difference from America is that the British do not have long senate investigations on the suitability of nominees for public office. I am rather repelled by the way in which even very professional American journalists get hooked on the witch-hunts associated with these hearings. Often the journalists are themselves on large expense accounts. Some of the most censorious American journalists would not themselves pass tests for gentlemen. This complicated system means that the self-cleansing sometimes in the past (shall we say?) taken home boxes of paper clips from the office.

Still, the effect is that in America an "investigative" spirit spreads up and down through each newspaper, whereas in Britain it often does not. A surprising consequence is that in a heavy British newspaper the financial editor (whom the British, to the endless confusion of Americans, call the city editor) will often be an economist like me, more attuned to what is going on with the treasury knights than what is going on in business.

This has the very bad effect of letting British businesses get away for far too long with gross inefficiency. For example, nearly all American businessmen are fortunately moved by what is happening to the price of their stock in the market; they live with the terror that their bonds will no longer be rated triple A. The financial comment for American media stems from New York and the political comment from Washington. In Britain, chairmen of quite large companies do not know the price of their shares at any particular moment, or even how far it has changed in the past week. These chairmen generally live in London and are more closely geared to what the government is doing to the economy than to what is happening to their business. When they meet a journalist like me at an embassy cocktail party, our conversation will probably be on when the Chancellor of the Exchequer is at last going to cut the surcharge on employers' national insurance contributions.

A good effect is that top British journalists are less liable than top American journalists to talk or accept rubbish about energy policy or even more important matters. As an example, consider what happened at the time of the Club of Rome's first booklet on "Limits to growth." This drew up a model on the assumption that recoverable supplies of all named minerals would be equal to five times known reserves, and that there would then be no supplies available for use. Every British economic editor could say at once that the supply curve of no material was of that shape. None of the metals was "used" in the way the model supposed; instead, metals are put in the shape of a car, and available for reuse when that car becomes clappered out. Some of the minerals concerned were part of the earth's crust, with supplies several million times larger than the model supposed. Most important, if this model had been right (which it was not), the world would have come to an end if any production continued at all; if we continued with production at the present level it would end in X years, and if everybody in the world halved his consumption for the sake of conservation it would end in 2X years.

The booklet used the method of drawing a chart on which one line (called existing economic growth) turned down catastrophically while still on the page, because "five times' existing reserves" were then "used" up, while another and lower line called something like "recommended growth" ran on off the page and was made to appear as a road to Utopia. The meaning of the chart depended on the breadth of the page; the "catastrophic fall" point on that second curve came beyond the right-hand side of the page, and the satisfying effect was achieved by using a pair of scissors on the computer printout.

If this sort of graphics had been displayed in a prospectus asking for money, its computers would have gone to prison. Almost every British economic editor said so, but among American journalists the booklet was widely believed, and in some American schools this rubbish is still taught.

Oddly, the British tradition of broader competence in general economic knowledge—but less daring professionalism in disturbing particular hornets' nests—has been strengthened by what has followed from the original monopoly in British broadcasting granted to the BBC. During my first six years as a journalist (1949–55), this had hilariously awful consequences. My editor at the time, Geoffrey Crowther, gave a series of radio talks which attracted one of the biggest audiences of any such talks up to that time. The series had to be stopped early, because both political parties (the Conservatives and Labour) said that the talks breached the BBC's charter by being deliberately critical of each of them (and unduly favourable to the other protester), and each demanded equal rights of reply. At one stage, the BBC monopoly even seemed on the point of accepting MPs' arrogant demand for a 14-day-rule, under which no subject was supposed to be debated on the BBC if it was expected to be debated within the next 14 days in Parliament. Although this demand was dropped under strong press criticism, there is an odd hangover to this day. Television channels are a little wary of running documentaries on important partisan issues likely to come immediately before Parliament (or else they run such programs in the most boring and unwatchable way, by having equal numbers of Labour and Tory MPs shout short accusatory sentences at each other). Instead, the best producers on all television channels prefer to run documentaries on deeper, less immediate, and less partisan subjects, such as energy policy.

When commercial television companies started their competition after 1955, these companies were told that their profitable contracts would be renewed only if they satisfied a review committee consisting of intellectually worthy people. All channels therefore upgrade both their entertainment shows and their talk shows above the level of taste of the proletariat, reaching the level of taste of such committees. Accordingly, British television is often regarded as the best in the world by worthly intellectuals found sitting on review committees. Consequently, except when sport is on the screens, the programs are therefore above the heads of young Hackney skinheads and Brixton blacks, so these go out and bash each other and burn up the inner cities. This is rather misleadingly called "British television's unique contribution to uplifting the national culture," but it does help to provide some sophisticated talk shows on energy policy.

I disagree with one sentence in our guidelines which suggests that comment may be more informed if people like energy correspondents are allowed to stay long on one beat. My experience is that any energy correspondent, farming correspondent, or whatever who stays long on one beat becomes a captive to his sources and to pressure groups like public relations officers. The system on my newspaper is to have a group of trained economists who have some overriding editing responsibility on specialist subjects where economic howlers might creep in. I came down from Cambridge University to *The Economist* with first-class honors in economics in 1949, and had mercifully short beats as a banking correspondent, a trade-union correspondent, a political correspondent, a defence correspondent, a decolonizing-of-the-British-Empire correspondent, and an antitown-planning correspondent. I was then made an assistant editor (economics), and told: "Watch out for copy in your old fields which misses economic points, or which swallows public relations officers' guff. As viewspaper editors we must always be flying the jolly roger, and public relations officers are our natural prey."

There is a particular danger if broadcasting bodies like the BBC acquire specialist correspondents on anything, because they soon become mouthpieces for public relations men. This is why the monstrous starving of funds from the BBC has not been as dreadful as many of us feared it might be. The BBC finances itself by a fixed licence fee from each viewer, which is raised only when the government agrees. A fixed licence fee is especially cramping when inflation is rampant, but when inflation is rampant the government is least willing to put it up. In order to escape from government pressures, the BBC will have to start accepting some advertisements (whose price rises with inflation). Everybody knows this, but anybody who says it is put in the establishment doghouse, especially by the BBC. Which leads us to:

Media Culture and Media Financing

With permission, I will take these two subjects together. This is an advantage because nobody can say anything numerately sensible about media financing in Britain. All British newspaper properties are a mixture of some assets, some extraordinary inefficiencies, and huge individual money-losers. When a tycoon called Sir Roger Moneybags buys them, he knows that he could make a bomb if he were to keep the rest of the properties and close down the inefficiencies and big money-losers. However, when he does buy them, pressure is put on him to promise faithfully that he will not make such closures. He usually intends to break this promise, but a strange mixture of establishment pressures and trade-union pressures plus the granting of other goodies (like part-ownership of profitable TV channels) then locks him in, he keeps the money-losers going on for a long time, is made Lord Moneybags in recognition of this, and the whole packet is sold after his death by his son to a new tycoon who repeats the whole process. During all of this, run-down losses actually made by the most deficit-ridden newspapers are hidden by being called overheads of more profitable parts of the group. This is why no newspapers' accounts should be believed. Statements that a particular newspaper lost 4 million pounds or made a small but positive profit last year, can be made equally truthfully or untruthfully after reading the same set of accounts.

By these means the British have kept in being three quality Sunday newspapers, when the most economic course would be to merge them into one highly profitable quality Sunday newspaper. If there were a monopoly Sunday newspaper, it might expand almost to the volume of American Sundays, which foreigners find difficult to carry, let alone read. As there are three, they are kept to moderate bulk, and surprisingly, they have gravitated towards the same sort of centrist views. This is because quite a large proportion of their readership also reads one or both of the other two, and they do not want to antagonize those readers by seeming shrill, inexpert, or too far outside the established view.

Probably, all three newspapers would deny this. Formally, *The Observer* is the one on the left. It used to be said of it that it could only be read with satisfaction by somebody who was "black, homosexual, and currently in prison for a good cause." Actually, it moved long ago to the center. This happened before it was rescued last time but one by an American oil company which preserved it rather like you might preserve seals in the Arctic, and before it was rescued this most recent time by the builder of a big multinational who was once accused by a Conservative prime minister of representing "the unacceptable face of capitalism." Indeed, rescues by right-wing proprietors probably turn expert journalists slightly farther to the left in defense. Proprietorial influence on papers in Britain is less prevalent than foreigners (or those who remember the Beaverbrook era) think.

The right-wing quality Sunday is the *Sunday Telegraph*. Its parent, the

Daily Telegraph, has long been the best-off of the quality daily newspapers because most quality-newspaper-readers are rich enough to be slightly right-wing. So the *Daily Telegraph* gained from the *Times,* which was hit by the growth of the *Financial Times*, and the best-written (but slightly more left-wing) Guardian did not attract the doctors and branch bank managers who read the *Daily Telegraph*. But the *Sunday Telegraph* found that one did not make most money among the quality Sundays by being the most right-wing.

The largest of the quality Sundays is the *Sunday Times*, which probably has the tradition of being the shrewdest recruiter of staff. It has been hampered because of the losses made by the *Times*, a paper which built up too large an establishment and has found difficulty in resolving its trade-union troubles. The *Times* group has now been bought by the most efficient of the press tycoons, Australia's Rupert Murdoch, with all the usual conditions and all the usual economic prospects.

Other Influences on Opinion

This has been a very incomplete chapter. It has not dealt with subjects which some would regard as central to the topic, such as:

1. Britain's popular, mass circulation, national dailies and Sundays. I do not think these have had a great effect on complicated issues like energy policy. This might have been a temporary accident. In the 1950s and 1960s the largest and most dynamic of the mass circulation dailies was the *Daily Mirror*, which gave general and politically important support to the Labour party, although in an idiosyncratic way (its leading lights had feuds with Harold Wilson). It is possible to imagine circumstances in which the *Daily Mirror* could have been an important leader of opinion in favor of "new look" policies such as excessive environmentalism or opposition to nuclear power. But by the time of the energy crisis, the *Daily Mirror* was struggling to avoid losing circulation to Rupert Murdoch's well-targeted and well-produced *Sun*. In the middlebrow section of the market, the *Daily Mail* (broadly pro-Thatcherite and pro-free-market) is temporarily better written and more dynamic than the less predictable *Daily Express*. So among the populars there has been no powerful voice during the energy crisis in favor of trying to repeal the laws of supply and demand.
2. Provincial dailies, evenings, and weeklies. These have gained through the restrictive practices of Fleet Street. The printing unions stop new technology from being used economically in London papers, but now evening papers can be started up with economic use of it in provincial towns or commuter areas. The National Union of Journalists prevents some new journalists from coming straight into good jobs in Fleet Street, so some of the brightest youngsters have to spend a probationary period in the provinces. The level of economic reporting in some provincial papers like the *Birmingham Post* is now very good indeed. But Britain is so understandably London-centerd that the provincials have not had much effect on Whitehall-dominated

government policy. As some of the brightest people on those papers are aiming eventually at Fleet Street jobs, they have tended to keep in the mainstream of the Fleet Street policy ethos. The editor of the local newspaper is not an important person in a local British community in the sense that he is in a local American community. That brings this chapter to its final and maybe most important point.

3. Lack of regionalism in Britain compared with the continent-wide United States. In an American snowbelt town there will be fairly unanimous support for cheap heating oil among the local newspapermen, newspaper readers, and politicians. This is how pressure groups win support in favor of trying absurdly to repeal the laws of supply and demand. America also has a system where lawyers can exercise extraordinary powers of delay through the courts. Any environmentally objectionable scheme will be fought through the courts, with huge publicity especially for the area affected. In Britain, matters cannot so easily be brought to court, and if an appeal is made from one court to another that matter becomes *sub judice*. Editors are in some ways inhibited in expressing views designed to prejudice the next court. More usually, an inspector will be sent down from London to hear local complaints against some environmentally-sensitive project. The local inhabitants may well greet him with a noisy demonstration, but they will not usually receive a favorable national press unless their complaints sound obviously logical.

There is one exception to this British rule of "no great regional solidarity," and it does affect energy policy. In most of the old coal mining areas, such as South Wales, there is great regional solidarity, partly because coal mining has made these areas so horrid that nobody else goes to live there. Many of the coal mines in the oldest areas are now quite uneconomic, but the National Coal Board is too frightened of local disturbances to close them down. That is why Britain has some of the most expensive coal in the world, and it now considers itself very lucky because from the North Sea it is pumping out some of the most expensive oil in the world, also. But there is not any great new regional feeling within the oil area in the cold north-east of Scotland (despite the brief flourishing of the Scottish Nationalist Party, crying "it's Scotland's oil"), and there is also not yet any great antagonistic feeling from the rest of the country against it. The picture in the press is of brave, hardy, if deservedly well-paid, strong men on oil rigs.

A regional split may be appearing in Britain, on much broader and worrisome grounds. It is noticeable that safe Conservative parliamentary seats in the south of England and safe Labour parliamentary seats in the rest of the kingdom have for some time been getting safer. That has been happening even though many Tory voters are unhappy that Mrs. Thatcher's Tory party has been swinging more to the right and most Labour voters are unhappy that Mr. Foot's Labour party has been swinging more to the left. Into this situation has come the new Social Democrat-Liberal alliance, which might either have astonishing electoral success (and wide press support and tacit television channel support) or else (even with that support) might come in second practically everywhere. In order to stop the geographical split from widening and perverting British government, I have for some time believed that Britain would be wise before or in the 21st century to build a new capital city like Washington or Canberra, somewhere in northern England like on some wilderness in Yorkshire. Many of the things I have said in this chapter will be unpopular with, and hotly denied by, my closest professional colleagues who are London journalists. This last point is meant to bring closing dissension nicely to the boil.

NINE

Institutions: A Discussion

Nelson Smith
Leonard J. Theberge

At the Harvard Business School in July 1979, a group of reporters and editors gathered to discuss the topic "Energy and the Press: Caught in the Middle." One of the participants, Eileen Shanahan of the now defunct *Washington Star*, observed, "I think we're all doing a lousy job, but only because the problem is so hard." If energy were simply another difficult journalistic assignment, chances are it would have been covered better. Newspeople are a hardy lot, and they seem to relish digging into a new and challenging subject. There was something about energy in the 1970s, however, that confounded them, caused them to chase after scapegoats, and sent them spinning their wheels.

This book has examined two specific issues, oil and nuclear power, and has found major problems with the press coverage of both. With regard to oil, it appears that the media, particularly in the United States, belabored the conspiracy theory long after it had been discredited. The real economic issues of the oil crisis were only addressed in some substantive fashion in the late 1970s, and then mainly in the print media. Nuclear power was largely ignored by major U.S. media organizations until the Three Mile Island accident. Coverage of the development of other energy sources could be criticized in much the same way: coal, natural gas, solar, gasohol, synfuels, and other alternative energy sources have been treated as either fads or panaceas. Media coverage of these energy sources has often exhibited the same lack of economic assessment and risk-balancing that has characterized oil and nuclear coverage.

Why did energy issues in the 1970s present news organizations with such travail? An understanding of the institutions as well as the issues might help

138

to illuminate the discussion. Take, for example, the problem of weak economic analysis in early reporting on the oil crises. Although it is true that network news organizations were simply understaffed in terms of economic reporters, the main problem seems to have been structural: no matter what the expertise of the reporter on the beat, it was filtered through layers of producers and editors who had little understanding of the economic forces at work, and was then broadcast by political reporters on White House or Capitol Hill assignments. The subtleties of economic policy were sacrificed to an organization chart which favored political coverage.

Another institutional problem in press coverage of energy was demonstrated by the participants at Ditchley Park in their discussion of the origins of the "conspiracy theory." News organizations, flushed with their success at ferreting out Watergate criminals, chose to rely upon the same techniques of "investigative journalism" in reporting the first oil crisis. The assumption was widespread among members of the press that enough legwork and digging would eventually reveal the culprit responsible for gas lines and escalating prices. However, what had worked so superbly in reportting the Watergate story turned out to be inappropriate for covering the complicated crisis in oil supply.

A recent study by The Media Institute, "TV Coverage of the Oil Crises: How Well Was the Public Served?," found that government-oriented solutions (rationing, mandatory conservation, price controls) received three times the coverage of nongovernment, market-oriented solutions. The government was the largest single source of information on network evening news programs with 56 percent, while outside experts were the sources of information only 2 percent of the time. The networks used government figures to discuss solutions 77 percent of the time, while oil industry sources were called upon only 9 percent of the time. The role of the government's policies, which contributed to the shortages, was largely ignored as the networks blamed OPEC and the oil companies.[1]

In examining these findings, it is possible to conclude that individual reporters were biased against oil companies or suspicious of OPEC, and that they covered the oil crises according to their own prejudices. A more realistic evaluation, though, would remove the onus from most individual reporters—who did their best to cover a difficult story objectively—and place it once again on the institutions for which they worked. The discussions at Ditchley Park revealed a cozy relationship between the permanent press establishment and the "permanent" bureaucracy in the U.S. and British governments, and that kind of relationship inevitably led to press reliance on government sources.

In the following pages based on the proceedings of the Ditchley Park conference, participants focus mainly on the coverage of energy. But in digesting their comments, the reader should understand that they are speaking of a great case history of economic coverage in the video age. The 1970s afforded mass media their first opportunity to report, comprehensively and over a long period of time, on a major sector of the international economy—the production and distribution of crude oil and refined products. Their performance in that test has implications for all future economic issues. In an age where news will increasing emanate from complex technological subjects, it is important that news organizations adjust their operations in accordance with the lessons learned from energy coverage. Indeed, there are already a number of encouraging signs that this change is taking place.

Since 1973, television networks have increased their capabilities in terms of both personnel and content. Each of the U.S. networks has at least one full-time economics correspondent; economic stories are played at the beginning of the broadcast with a wide variety of arresting video sequences; and computer graphics and other techniques are being used to spruce up dull economic stories so they will hold the viewer's attention.

Press and Policy

In Norman Macrae's chapter on British press institutions, it was asserted that journalists in the United Kingdom need only convince a small group of ministers and civil servants in order to exert profound influence on national policy. The relationship between press, people, and government is different for each of the countries that was discussed at Ditchley Park, but in a variety of ways, it became clear that there is a cross-influence among all three sectors in each country.

THOMAS BETHELL: In Washington, there seems to me to be a kind of natural symbiosis between the bureaucracy and the press. The bureaucracy is there all the time, I mean for years, whereas the administration changes nowadays every four years. The lower-down members of the bureaucracy are able to influence policy—to create policy, in fact—by short-circuiting the people who are above them in the agencies and going straight to the *Washington Post*. . . . My impression is that in England, the civil servants do not have to use the newspapers to influence the ministers because they control them completely anyway.

TOM BURKE: One has seen in Britain, over the last two administrations, a considerable amount of leaking to the press from lower down in the civil service. You have an institutionalized sort of leaking to the press politically in Britain through the lobby system, the lobby correspondents, which is a sort of formal way of leaking government positions.

JOHN F. O'LEARY: I think first of all you have to regard the dealings of my colleagues as essentially manipulative. They don't seek merely to impart truth to Congress, to a newspaperman, to a television reporter, or to the public when they appear in the media. They seek to impart a point of view.

JEFF GREENFIELD: That's a terribly useful point Mr. O'Leary makes. When people come to the press, whether it's Ralph Nader, Herb Schmertz, or Senator Jackson, there's a transaction one has to understand. With very few exceptions, mainstream reporters—the kind that report on TV news and in print—do not, I believe, have the same motive of manipulation. They may come to very bad conclusions, but the role playing they go through is, "I'm trying to sift through this and figure it out as best I can. I know they're all manipulating me; now, who do I think is more credible?" I know Herb Schmertz is trying to get me to like Mobil better; I know Senator Jackson wants me to vote for him for President; I know Ralph Nader wants contributions to "Congress Watch." But I'm not sure what Dan Rather wants, except for me to watch his program.

RICHARD L. DUNHAM: Another way the press affects policy is that press reports have a very pronounced effect on the way government officials react. For example, in the White House, it's standard procedure every day to circulate excerpts from the print media and TV news shows. And every bureaucrat and government official tends to look at press clips to see if he was successful in getting his point across—and if not, what steps can he take to countermand what might have been a negative impression.

THOMAS UKERT: It's hard to assess the real impact, though. In Germany, a couple of years ago, we ran a small opinion survey to find out how a group of opinion leaders forms its views on energy matters. And we found out that they take news from the newspapers, from the TV and radio, but if they are really interested in learning about the topic, they get in touch with the person they think really knows about the situation and ask him to explain it.

ADRIAN HAMILTON: I think the answer is that the press and television helped to raise the consciousness of the public which had been aroused by the actuality of shortages or pretended shortages. The press tends to confirm the conventional view at any one time of the nature of the energy crisis that you would expect. In Britain, the press tends to influence policy-making on very specific questions, when it pushes hard on something that is obviously of public concern—but I doubt whether history would have been any different if there had been no press.

TOM BURKE: I'd agree with the substance of what Mr. Hamilton said. The media influenced policy at the margin—around precise bits of policy. And it's influenced public opinion probably very little, except in the sense of putting something on the agenda. In the nuclear debate, for instance, I think the influence of the media has simply been to get people to take a view; it hasn't had a great deal of influence on what that view actually is.

JOHN F. O'LEARY: I think that the most important contribution the press has made to the current energy position of the United States was its effect on general social attitudes, beginning in the early seventies—the sort of thing that followed on Rachel Carson's pesticides expose, for example. The media picked up that theme time and time again. All the coverage of environmental despoliation led to a sea change in our attitudes toward environmental control on the one hand, and on the other, toward individual access to decision-making. That's been a revolutionary change in the last decade, and it's large-ly been a product of the media.

JEAN PELLERIN: In my opinion, the sharp rise in the price of energy had much more effect on people than the news. So there is probably more influence coming from the government than from other sources.

ROGER PETERSON: Speaking for television, I think the only impact that oc-curred at the beginning of the oil crisis in '73 was probably a harmful one for television reporting itself. The audience saw how confused we were and how little we know about the problem. Over the years, we've educated ourselves as well as our audience—but whether there has been major impact, I don't know.

HERBERT SCHMERTZ: I think the impact of the media is basically short-term. Radio and television reports can have a very immediate effect on policy. But over a period of time, rational policies will overcome the influence of radio and television.

CLAUDE G. PONCELET: In general, public attitudes or public opinion on energy issues is very volatile, and also very short-lived. People's interest in energy issues—and therefore, their willingness to be informed about energy issues—varies substantially with time, and really depends on major news events. For example, in the United States, the various incidents such as the oil crises, the coal miners' strike, the Three Mile Island accident, the natural gas shortage that occurred several years ago—all these have led the public to express a great of concern about energy. And in those times, the polls show 50 to 80 percent of the people expressing such concern. But I was appalled to see, in September 1981, a poll showing only 7 percent of the peo-ple in the U.S. expressing any concern about energy.

ROBERT S. GORALSKI: A word of caution about public opinion polls, though. I remember one poll showing 65 percent of Americans did not believe there was a real energy crisis, which led me to conclude that two out of three Americans simply thought it was the oil companies that contrived it. But when you studied the regional breakdown, you found that the people in Boston and New York responded the same way as the people in Dallas and Houston. Sixty-five percent of the people in Dallas and Houston did not believe there was an energy crisis for different reasons than people in the nor-theast; they felt that if the *government* just got out of the way, the shortages would go away. The figures were totally misleading.

And when you look at the influence of television . . . there is one survey with figures each year on how many people get their news "primarily through television," and it's something like 68 percent now. Therefore, people say they get most of their news from television. But when further inquiry is made and they ask specifically, "How did you find out about a new leader in Iran? Where did you get a specific fact?," by and large, it is all from the newspapers. Overall, I think what people are saying is, "We had an impression from television, but the hard facts we get primarily from newspapers." So the question is, just how influential is television? Is it superficial? Is that what the viewer concludes?

JEFF GREENFIELD: I've just finished writing a book on the campaign for the presidency, which concludes that television was far less powerful in determining the outcome than the conventional wisdom would have dictated. And I notice Tom Bethell's study of inflation for The Media Institute, suggesting the networks subliminally blame everyone but the government for inflation. That study came out about the same time as a major poll taken in the U.S. for the New York Stock Exchange, which found that the overwhelming majority of Americans blame the government for the condition of the American economy. So that whatever one might think was produced by these studies, the public seems to filter them through its own expectations.

ALAN REYNOLDS: Well, no generalization can be fair, but as far as television news broadcasts go, they're not as important and influential as people think. If you count noses, sure, a lot of people watch them, but where opinions are formed among policy-makers the written media are far more important. For example, I was recently contacted by "The Today Show" about the gold standard of all things, because *Business Week* had broken two stories on the gold standard, and they figured this was now an issue. But the making of issues, the definition of an issue, very rarely in the economic arena originates in electronic media.

JOHN F. O'LEARY: But there's a fascinating kind of feedback to the news source itself with TV. I spent hundreds of hours before congressional committees in the spring of 1979 during the gas line crisis. And that, of course, was confrontational. The congressmen would attack me. We'd have long periods, a half-hour or an hour, in which we were simply exchanging views with the cameras off—then a Toby Moffett or Andy Maguire would come in and launch an attack, and as if by signal all the cameras in the room would go on; the temperature would rise significantly, and then that's what would be shown that evening. After those periods of confrontational discussions, I thought this was really no way of imparting information to the Congress. So, I arranged for a series of meetings with the same group of people, early in the morning. And we didn't discuss it with a lot of the media, since the media didn't show up. During those meetings, with 50 or 75 congressmen present, we could have an exchange of information that was honest, thoughtful and probing. An hour later I'd appear with the same cast in front of the cameras, and these guys would tear us apart: "Why is the government so stupid?"

"Why are the oil companies cheating?" and so on. The reason was really quite simple: the congressmen knew that the thing that goes on television and captures the American people is drama. It has nothing to do with the facts; it's entertainment.

CLAUDE G. PONCELET: I do think that news reporting on the nuclear issue has had an impact on the current situation of the nuclear power program in the United States—but I think it would be wrong to blame the media, to blame journalists alone, for this situation. To the extent that an issue is highly, visibly controversial, politicians tend to adopt a no-decision, "we'll do more studies" kind of stance. I do think, on the other hand, that the news media could improve its coverage—maybe by *not* covering so many of the small incidents related to minor releases of radiation that now tend to make national news, national headlines.

Media Organizations

Having looked at some of the ways in which the press exerts influence on events, let us turn to the factors within the press institutions themselves which tend to establish and direct that influence along certain paths. In the course of this inquiry, a number of different aspects will be considered: the individual journalists themselves, in terms of their role and their training; how the institutional habits of the organizations for whom they work tend to color the news they purvey; and finally, whether the press's long tradition of "balanced" reporting is still useful in this new age of information.

The Journalist

According to a recent study of media and business elites by Professors S. Robert Lichter and Stanley Rothman, the new journalist departs radically from the cigar-chomping "Front Page" stereotype of the past. The study found the media elite to be "a new leadership group that has arrived as a major force in American society" and demographically typical of other leadership groups: overwhelmingly white, male, highly educated, well-paid, and possessing a cosmopolitan outlook. The authors noted: "Yesteryear's ragtag muckrakers, who tirelessly championed the little guy against powerful insiders, have become insiders themselves."[2] If you think of this faintly *arriviste* fellow as an energy reporter, it's not surprising that he might appear to spend a lot of air time discussing government-oriented solutions to oil shortages. If, as Lichter and Rothman say, he is being "courted by politicians," it is no wonder he would turn to them for his explanations.

But whom do these new journalists talk *to*—whom do they perceive as their audience? In some sense, of course, the journalist who wishes to have an impact on policy will direct his work toward the center of influence, a target which is more recognizable in some countries than in others. Norman Macrae said at Ditchley Park: "During the '60s, if you got any economic view accepted by Sir Alec Cairncross* and about three others, it did basically go into British economic policy."

In the United States, where power is much more diffuse and the public exerts a much stronger and more direct influence on policy than in Great Britian, the journalist must find a less specific goal at which to direct his work. In his study of leading media organizations entitled *Deciding What's News*, Herbert Gans described the response of news people when asked who their real audience is:

> When I pressed the journalists for additional information about the actual audience, they indicated that it spanned all age, income, educational and other levels; but when I pressed still further, they described what in essence constituted their upscale audience. The magazine journalists saw their readers primarily as affluent and college-educated, with the men holding professional or managerial jobs.... Some television journalists thought that many of their viewers were older, but others could not understand why so many of the commercials featured denture adhesives and laxatives. Virtually all imagined their viewers to be basically middle-class.... In fact, I met only one television journalist who correctly saw the audience as consisting of persons mainly of working-class background.[3]

Here we have a well-educated group of reporters, writing and broadcasting to what they perceive to be a sophisticated audience. Why all the difficulty in reporting energy issues?

To be fair, part of the difficulty is just what Eileen Shanahan said: "the problem is so hard." Daniel Yergin, writing in the *Columbia Journalism Review*, called energy reporting "an unprecedented challenge to journalism." Yergin wrote:

> At the heart of the difficulty is the fact that the "energy problem" is not really one problem at all. It is a series of problems, some of them only tangentially related: storm windows, nuclear waste disposal, OPEC geopolitics, and sun rights. This creates a paradox. On the one hand, the number and complexity of these concerns means the reporters must specialize. On the other, it means that each news organization must be able to convey a sense of the problem *as a whole* to its readers and viewers, and this requires an editorial hand with a broad grasp of the entire political, economic, and technological story."[4]

The discussions at Ditchley Park revealed two characteristics of journalists. First, they seem unsure of just what role to play in the transaction of news. Is their responsibility that of an educator, or is that not the function of a journalist? Where does one draw the line? Second, they seem unsuited in some basic ways to cover a story as complicated as Yergin describes. Roger

---

* Sir Alex Cairncross served as head of the United Kingdom's Economic Service from 1964–1969.

Peterson correctly noted that television reporters "educated themselves" in the past decade. Should that training now be part of the standard curriculum?

ADRIAN HAMILTON: More and more, journalists are looking to write not for the reader, but for some other kind of audience, whether the Pulitzer Prize committee or their own contacts. And what worries me is *not* what worries a lot of people, which is that newspapers are too much about entertainment, too much about readers. What worries me is precisely the opposite. Newspapers and television are becoming more and more concerned about other constituencies — their colleagues, the prize-giving community, or other people commenting on them. And I find that disturbing.

ROGER PETERSON: I think we have to see journalists as educators. I think it's the function of journalism to educate, even when it's dull, and when the ratings are not what they should be, or circulation isn't boosted. Certain times, you have an obligation to present stories which are simply dull, and get them right. And the way television, in particular, has been going, it's moving in the opposite direction: a high regard for entertainment, for pictures, has just distorted the objectivity factor and suddenly has the capacity to educate.

THOMAS UKERT: Well, I think it's a rather hopeless venture to educate the public, because if there is no big event, no big price change or supply crisis, who is interested in the operating problems of the oil companies? Nobody. Even if every paper, every TV station would program that background information, nobody would listen, nobody would remember.

ANTHONY J. PARISI: I'd take that even further. I think we ought to leave the poor guy alone. I mean, the assumption is that the consumer simply must be informed on each and every issue that each and every one of us considers important. It's a hopeless task. One of the reasons you can't do that kind of education thing is that nobody wants it.

NORMAN MACRAE: The two colleagues I've felt most in rapport with here are Hans Kepplinger, who has an assiduous tabulation of facts, and Allan Reynolds, for his marvelous, irreverent free-market verve. But the ideal economic journalist is a mixture between the two — and I think America needs more Hans Kepplingers, seeing exactly what is happening as things proceed.

WILLIAM D. SMITH: American journalists are terrific. I was one, so I have to say that, but they are. Yet they do have a general failing which I don't think the British do. The ideal American journalist is someone who doesn't know anything. I quote Bob Woodward. He told me, "I don't want anyone who knows anything covering any important stories." We've carried that into economic journalism.

JAMES C. TANNER: Let's go back a moment to '73. Why weren't there any specialists or journalists knowledgeable about energy? Well, there were a few, a handful, mostly in the trade press. But there wasn't any audience, so you just didn't have many trained people in that area. Then when the roof fell in, obviously, untrained reporters were rushed into the breach. The traditional method of covering any developing news story, even for an untrained reporter, is to go to the experts. Well, I submit here and now that there are no real experts in energy, not even today. It's too much of a complicated area. There are many, many people who are experts in specific areas of energy, but I wonder if anyone in the world fully grasps all the complexities.

ALAN REYNOLDS: With many journalists, their training teaches them that reality is subjective, it's a matter of opinion. What we're skirting around is the issue of the *truth*. That is to say, if a journalist interviews John Kenneth Galbraith and me, one of us is wrong. (I can give you a hint as to which one it is.) And if you were to ask me how to fix that, I wouldn't say, "Send the journalist to an economics course." I'd say, "Send him to Professor Kelley and he'll teach him epistemology, standards of logic and evidence, so that you don't just report opinions and conclusions, you ask probing questions that get at 'what is your reasoning, Dr. Whatchamacallit?' and 'what is the evidence'?" And this is not a matter of professional consensus, either, because I can tell you that the Western world has been run on the professional consensus of economics for the past ten or twelve years, and that was a very serious mistake.

ISABEL MUHLFENZEL: TV is a very young thing, which presents a special problem there: we haven't enough trained people. There are so many news people in television who really aren't trained journalists at all.

JEFF GREENFIELD: In the U.S., the kind of people recruited to do the news, particularly in local markets, have become a source of great derision. They're known among the more serious journalists as "Harry Hairsprays," because they tend to be picked more for the quality of their hair or how they wear a blazer than for their news ability. . . .

HERBERT SCHMERTZ: My perception of the BBC is that they are more candid than the Amreican networks about their news operations. For example, when they do their evening news, the person doing it is referred to as a "reader" rather than a reporter.

TOM BURKE: Yes, the newscasters are not reporters or journalists. They're specifically there to be faces. As far as I know, the total program content is in the hands of the editors, not of the newscasters.

Institutional Habits

In May 1979, at the height of the controversy over oil companies' profits, President William Tavoulareas of Mobil Oil was called to testify before the Energy and Power Subcommittee of the House Interstate and Foreign Commerce Committee. Although there were some spirited exchanges in the course of committee questioning, the Mobil executive's testimony consisted largely of patient restatements of the company's position in defense of its profits. Reporters made dutiful notes of his comments. Occasionally the whirr of a TV camera could be heard, especially during hostile questioning from Representative Andrew Maguire, a prominent antagonist of the oil industry. However, there seemed to be no sustained, newsworthy story to be drawn from the day's appearance. Finally, the ranking Republican on the Subcommittee, Representative James Collins of Texas, excused Tavoulareas, and he rose from his seat to leave the room.

As he began to walk from the witness desk, though, Congressman Maguire seized the microphone and began shouting questions toward Tavoulareas, sarcastically calling him "Mr. President of Mobil Oil." Tavoulareas, perplexed by the breach of protocol, managed a quizzical smile and shrugged as he moved through the crowded spectator area and then out the door. Representative Collins reminded Maguire, with a rap of the gavel, that the "gentleman's time has expired."

When the incident began, one of the network reporters signalled to his crew; the hot lights when on, and the whirring cameras started up. That night, the reporter used Tavoulareas' exit as the centerpiece of a story on political contention over oil profits, and it played at the top of the broadcast. But from the editing, sound, and voice-over, it appeared to the viewer that Tavoulareas had walked out, grinning contemptuously, in the middle of a hearing—a conclusion at variance with reality. The reporter also included a brief shot of Tavoulareas whispering off-mike to his colleagues an alleged derogatory remark about Maguire. As TV drama, it was an exciting episode. The viewer saw an oilman and a consumerite congressman dueling in the sun. What the viewer did *not* get from the sketchy information that accompanied this video showdown was a grasp of why Mobil argued as it did, or more broadly, whether oil profits were excessive or not.

Why did a seasoned reporter make the wrongheaded editorial judgment to go with conflict instead of enlightenment? The answer lies partly with the reporter. He did a bad job that day, to be sure. But an additional answer lies in the institutional habits of his network, and in the demands of the medium itself. News has become a top-dollar item on television, and the three network evening news broadcasts are as bound up in the competition for ratings as any sit-com entertainment program. What wins ratings is drama and sensation, not thoughtfulness, and to stay competitive a network must express labyrinthian complexities in a way that grabs the viewer's attention.

The trend toward using entertainment in the delivery of news can be compared to putting sugar in breakfast cereal. Without it, TV people claim, the viewer will never consume the nourishing but boring data he needs in order to grow wise. To come extent, news organizations have to cater to the lowest common denominator, and that can turn even the most serious stories into Cocoa Puffs.

In his landmark work, *Public Opinion*, Walter Lippmann described how a Miss Sherwin of Gopher Prairie might understand reports of the First World War:

> She has never been to France, and certainly she has never been along what is now the battlefront. Pictures of French and German soldiers she has seen, but it is impossible for her to imagine three million men. Miss Sherwin has no access to the order of battle maps, and so if she is to think about the war, she fastens upon Joffre and the Kaiser as if they were engaged in a personal duel. Perhaps if you could see what she sees with her mind's eye, the image in its composition might be not unlike an eighteenth century engraving of a great soldier. He stands unruffled and more than life size, with a shadowy army of tiny little figures winding off into the landscape behind.[5]

If Miss Sherwin were still following current events when the energy crisis struck, she probably saw it in similarly personal terms: instead of Joffre and the Kaiser, it was Jimmy Carter versus the Ayatollah; or Ralph Nader versus J. R. Ewing . . . or Andy Maguire versus William Tavoulareas. In providing her with a simple and dramatic clash of personalities, the reporter described above was responding to her own tastes and capacities. In a medium so dependent on consumer reaction, to do otherwise means to miss the brass ring of ratings.

*   *   *

At Ditchley Park, journalists, academics, and business and government people discussed a variety of issues related to the institutional imperatives of media organizations. The picture that emerged was one of many talented, dedicated people trying to tackle a tough story, and being confounded by such concerns as ratings and budgets. The question of "event versus process" was touched upon often: What is the responsibility of journalists to inform the public about great issues when no crisis is occurring? How should the press help people to understand a sudden event like Three Mile Island before it happens?

*   *   *

ADRIAN HAMILTON: The object of a free market of information is to allow as many outlets as possible for people with alternative views. What's happening now is that newspaper monopolies are occurring in many American cities, and the number of newspapers is declining in Britain. And as there are only a few channels on television in Europe, there's an increasing feeling that maybe these outlets, whether it's the *New York Times* or the BBC, should somehow take in all the views that might otherwise have been represented by six different newspapers. . . .

JEFF GREENFIELD: The structure of the network news itself is governed in part by the fear that you will lose the audience if the structure of your news isn't exciting enough. That is, within that half-hour there's a concern about lengthy, abstract stories or stories without sufficiently interesting pictures. The theory is, unlike a newspaper where if you're bored by page one, you turn right to page four, and read the comics or the sports section, a network newscast has to be watched linearly. You have to start at the beginning and stay with it throughout the half hour. And if it bogs down at any point, you lose half your audience. Therefore, the argument goes, dull stories are subordinated to those which are more dramatic. So inflation stories are covered with shots of a supermarket when they tell you prices have gone up. Political coverage gets dominated by the campaign trail, because you can get pictures of balloons and crowds.

What this suggests is that the imperative to keep the audience, the fear of losing a single ratings point, tends to impinge on what the networks might do in the way of deeper or more serious journalism. And I'd be interested to know whether there's a corresponding tendency toward attention-getting news in the other countries we're talking about.

ISABEL MUHLFENZEL: The situation in Germany is somewhat comparable. If we make a special news program, then we have to get an audience. If our program shows a low rating, we have to change the program to catch a bigger audience.

MICHEL ANFROL: In France we have three networks, and the funding of the networks is quite special because Channel One, for instance, gets 66 percent of its budget from advertising and 34 percent from the national fee that's paid, like in Germany, by every TV owner. Channel Two gets 50–50 percent from advertising and fees and Channel Three gets 100 percent from fees—that's noncommercial television. And so there is some kind of competition between Channel One and Channel Two on the 8:00 p.m. evening news, because success for one of the channels means more advertising will be coming to it. Otherwise, for the in-depth reporting, what you might call the French version of "60 Minutes," I would say that we don't much care about the audience ratings. Usually we go on the air at 9:30 p.m., sometimes 10:00 or 10:30 p.m., and we get five percent or two percent ratings, but we don't really care. If it's something very important, we might move that "60 Minutes" type show to 8:30 p.m., and then we get 18 or 20 percent of the ratings. But there's no impact on the news personnel.

ISABEL MUHLFENZEL: I should point out that there's a big difference between how we make news in Europe, especially in Germany, and how news is made in the United States. Our German news program is much, much bigger—there's a larger percentage of shows presenting news. This means not only news *per se*, but commentaries, editorials, features, documentaries, and so on . . . . And a word about our structure and funding. Everyone, as M. Anfrol pointed out, who has a TV set has to pay a certain fee to the post office. Every station has a board of advisors. Each program is supported by several of the stations. So, for instance, Bavaria, which I belong to, supports one program 20 percent; Hamburg supports it 38 percent; Cologne with 25 percent, and so forth. We get a variety of opinions because, of course, Bavaria is more conservative, Hamburg is less so, and there's a mix. So the viewer knows when a program comes from Munich he gets another angle than a show from Cologne, and as long as we can show all these different angles, the viewer can decide which he likes better.

ANTHONY J. PARISI: I think there's an assumption that our overly commercial networks in the States suffer by comparison because of our commercial competition. As a relatively new resident of the U.K., it's my observation that the evening news, the spot news coverage by the U.S. networks is better than that in Britian. I mean, all these little gimmicks that are used do actually increase my interest in the coverage. I'm appalled at the static image I find on the BBC evening broadcast. I guess I'd have to admit that I'm complimenting "show business" . . . but I also think that the issues are covered as well, if not better, by Cronkite and Rather than I see now on the BBC.

ROGER PETERSON: As far as the "gimmicks" Tony's talking about are concerned, it *is* show business, but at the same time, it allows stories to get on that five or six years ago were being kissed off. You'd come in with a script on economics or business, they'd say, "What pictures do you have? No pictures? OK, maybe 45 seconds we'll take, maybe 30 seconds—or maybe just summarize it and we'll have the anchorman read it." Now, we're able to do so much with these wonderful machines they have in the control room that baffle me, we can get a good, substantial story on the air.

JEFF   GREENFIELD: Yes,   you're   talking   about   computer-generated graphics—they go under names like "Quantel" and "Kyron 4." It sounds like *Star Wars*, but essentially, they're machines that enable you to take static images and make them visually interesting. And to me, some of those "gimmicks" are no different from the fact that the *Times* of London no longer runs classified ads on the front page. There's nothing wrong with it. I think the look of a TV news show ought to be considered in the same way that page make-up is in print. I don't consider that "show-biz." It's a perfectly legitimate way to appeal to an audience.

WILLIAM D. SMITH: Agreeing with what's been said, something still bothers me about this. What I saw happen at the *New York Times* was that in an attempt to make it more interesting, the make-up people took over the Sunday financial section of the paper and moved it from something we put together on a Thursday night, which was pertinent, to something we put together a week and a half in advance, that nobody reads. And I wonder if the gimmicks and prettying up in television might take over the momentum and push out the hard news. I think that tension, that push to really report the hard news has to come from the reporters themselves. Don't let the show-biz stuff intrude on the hard news.

ROBERT S. GORALSKI: I think that's already a very serious problem. The ratings race leads to horrible distortions. A good example: AP now has three reporters covering the war in Afghanistan from outside the country, and they move a story on the war across the wires every day. There are hundreds of casualties each day, reports from people coming out of Kabul, diplomats interviewed by AP. It's a major war going on out there. When did you last see anything on American television about Afghanistan? There are no pictures, and therefore AP is ignored by the networks because they have no pictures to go along with the facts.

JEFF GREENFIELD: True, but then you get back to the structural problem I was pointing out earlier. If the *Los Angeles Times* wants to run an 8000 word take-out, let's say on energy resources, they don't expect everyone is going to read it. They are not going to lose their readership because the story starts on page one and three hours later you get to the end. But a TV producer has to put on every story with the expectation that every viewer will have some interest in looking at it, because he can't avoid it.

CLAUDE G. PONCELET: The one criterion I have heard so far is that it has to be interesting. Let me suggest that in terms of forming public opinion, the viewer receives various messages: the messge that comes to the conscious mind and a very potent nonverbal message that comes to the subconscious mind. And I think public opinion is formed, to a large extent, in the subconscious mind. I wonder what is the relevance of this aspect of nonverbal communication?

ROBERT L. DUPONT: The act of watching television, including the news, is different for people who watch it a lot from people who watch it a little. People who watch television news infrequently tend to watch it with their eyes right on the set. They are very careful to observe what's happening. People who watch television a lot, and here I am describing the most typical TV viewers, don't sit and stare at the set; they're often engaged in other activities with the television set on. They are tuning their attention in and out. What is largely conveyed in that case by most TV watching, is an emotional impression. This is very different from the print media. When we talk about pictures, that is what we're talking about. There is a kind of tone or value, a sense you get from television. If one is interested in information, one is less likely to get it from the television experience than from print for at least two reasons. First, reading requires more work and second something that is read can be reviewed. Both characteristics, the effort of attention and review are important parts of learning. TV conveys feelings: print conveys facts.

HANS MATHIAS KEPPLINGER: In West Germany's 1976 election campaign, we found that those who were heavy viewers of television increasingly thought that the liberal coalition would win—in spite of the fact that if you asked "Who will you vote for?," nothing changed over the whole period. So we tried to find out why people thought the liberals would win. We found that only those who viewed television often received that impression. So we first tried to analyze the verbal content and didn't get an interesting result. Then I started to make content analyses of the shooting and cutting techniques. We analyzed what was said about the chances of the candidates, and found basically no difference in what was said about the candidates of the left and right in terms of verbal content. But in the nonverbal content, we found several times as many pictures showing disapproval toward the Conservatives' candidate as there were toward the Liberals' candidate. There was a clear bias in the pictures. The Conservative candidate was shown as a losing man with booing audiences and people who were not interested in what he was saying, while the Liberal coalition candidate was shown with approving audiences of very interested people. An English research crew with whom we worked found that the showing of approval or disapproval is very effective in creating the image of a bad man or a good man. And this is used very often in television and most people don't know it.

TOM BURKE: I'm not sure what that tells me, though. Maybe people were always booing Strauss and applauding Schmidt . . . . But I wanted to bring up another aspect of the relationship between pictures and the story itself. Sometimes the media actually *creates* events because it needs photos. During the riots this summer in English cities, there were a number of cases where television camera crews—most, I think, not from Britain—quite specifically encouraged people to create pictures. There was a fair amount of scandal about that. And it seems to me that the competitive pressures we have been talking about will inevitably lead to that sort of thing. It's a very worrying prospect.

ADRIAN HAMILTON: The same thing was true of the disturbances over the hunger strikers in Northern Ireland. There were at least three incidents which were taped by Americans where they actually got people to throw stones at troops. And what was very clear was that all the crews arrived with instructions from a producer telling them, "Well, what we want is a story about a society going under," and they went out to find that society. What worried me was not so much the actual faking, but the deliberate selection of incidents to illustrate a story they'd already decided on before they had left New York.

JEFF GREENFIELD: At CBS, if a reporter is involved in urging on violence just to get good footage, it is cause for instant dismissal.

ROGER PETERSON: That's ABC's policy too.

MICHEL ANFROL: Well, I covered a KKK rally in Texas, a cross-burning against the Vietnamese refugees in Houston, and I must tell you that before they started the cross-burning, the people there asked if every TV crew was ready.

JEFFREY GREENFIELD: That's different—if you're saying people are sensitive to the arrival of the media, there's no doubt about that.

HERBERT SCHMERTZ: Oh, there's an enormous manipulation of television. Having worked in political campaigns, I know that the scheduling of the candidate each day is designed to get him to a spot where TV can get a good visual shot by 10:30 a.m. so it can be transmitted back to New York and onto the evening news. And the demonstrations we have talked about, on nuclear power, for example, are planned and carried out because they know the television producers love these kinds of things for the evening news. For example; the announcements of demonstrations such as Ralph Nader's Big Business Day in 50 cities. The press release goes out, the cameras gear up, 20 people may show up, but when it gets on television it looks like a much larger demonstration than it was. There is a substantial amount of manipulation because everybody now knows what you all are looking for.

JEFF GREENFIELD: But the startling thing in political campaign coverage now is the degree to which the reporters will *tell* you that the candidates are trying to manipulate the media. In fact, it has gone almost overboard. When President Carter went to the Italian market in Philadelphia, all the reporters said, "This is a media event you are seeing." My hope is that the candidates will now give this up.

ANTHONY J. PARISI: It seems to me a fair medium would allow itself to be manipulated by both sides.

* * *

LEONARD J. THEBERGE: Applying this strong orientation toward coverage of events to business and economic news, I want to ask the panel how this affects the content of news? Does it alter the individual's understanding in some significant way?

TOM BURKE: As someone who seeks to manipulate the media and use the media to educate people, my feeling is that the event orientation chiefly of television, but also to some extent of print media, actually creates a very distorted impression of some complex issues like nuclear power. For example, after an event like Three Mile Island, the whole debate centered around safety. But, safety is only one issue in a very substantial package of issues. People who are critics of nuclear power may make up their own judgments with a completely different set of emphases across the spectrum from something like low-level radiation, which is a highly scientific issue, to nuclear proliferation or civil liberties, which are highly political issues. Now, whether any of that actually gets seen by the public at large depends on whether there's an event that will let you present that issue as part of the package. So if the Israelis blow up an Iraqi reactor, you can get people thinking about proliferation and the relationship of power stations and proliferation. But you constantly get this sort of false perspective of that basis people are to make judgments on.

DAVID KELLEY: Economic events tend to be changes or alterations in underlying price movements or supply developments or what have you. If you are not in the field or even in business at all, they tend to mean nothing. To someone outside business, the business pages are hopelessly dull. But they can take on a greater interest if some context is provided, which is what we have been calling a "process" story. My impression, from reading the *New York Times* for 10 or 15 years, is that there are now relatively more of these stories on all subjects—perhaps because television now provides the headlines. Is it impossible for television to pick up an issue like natural gas pricing, in between congressional hearings and shortages and so forth, the way newspapers do?

ALAN T. GREGORY: I wouldn't draw the distinction between television and print in this case, but between the "pop" press and the "posh" press. You are talking about straightforward commercial operations. For example, if you take the *Times* of London and the *Financial Times* in Britain, their audience and the kind of audience which they hope to maintain and increase is one to which you can address "educative" programs outside the events that make hot news. But if you go to the "pop" press and the television media who are looking for audiences of several million, well, I'm afraid you can't expect the media to produce educative material in between crisis events. It's just a fact of life.

ROBERT S. GORALSKI: But somewhere along the line, you've got to go out of your way and say, "It's a dull story but I think people ought to know about it." Fred Friendly said the role of television is to raise the level of consciousness, and you don't do this by only reporting crises. You've got to raise the level of consciousness by getting stories *before* they become crises.

JEFF GREENFIELD: If you define television broadly enough to include public television and cable, you can find in-depth coverage of all kinds of complicated events. There's C-SPAN, a cable channel that covers the House of Representatives and political speeches. Nobody watches them, but it's covered. A two-hour debate between Ralph Latt and Ralph Nader on nuclear power was presented on prime-time public TV a year ago. I would guess the ratings were much worse than the French debate on nuclear power. But if one is serious about saying there has to be room on television for non-crisis reporting of significant events, you then begin to raise, I think, the most fundamental question about whether you can somehow compel television to be responsible. Networks have wanted an hour news program for the last six years in the United States; the local stations will not give it to them, and the networks won't take half an hour out of prime time entertainment to put it on. I suspect an hour newscast would take away a large part of the excuse the networks now have not to cover things in-depth. The question is, "If it's a fair judgment that the public doesn't want it, what kind of counterweight is there for the networks to expand their coverage?" I assume nobody wants the government to compel the American television networks to carry more news....

ROBERT S. GORALSKI: Encapsulation of the news is always criticized, but actually, most critics seem to find it's the longer stories on "60 Minutes" and "20/20" that are worse than the 90-second spots. And there, they don't have the deadline problem.

HERBERT SCHMERTZ: I resent the idea that deadline pressure is any kind of excuse for shoddy reporting. It is not written that a story which is incomplete has to go to press. It is not written that reporters or the public have to be victims of the technology of television, and it's not written anywhere that there's some immutable law that they must oversimplify. If they choose to do that, which is their prerogative, then they should admit to the public that that's precisely what they're doing. Then the public can make a judgment as to whether what they're getting is useful in making rational judgments or is nonsense.

* * *

Balance

In a recent advertisement for ABC News, correspondent Peter Jennings was quoted on the subject of truth: "There is no one single truth. Because the truth of the Israeli settler who is leaving the Sinai, and the truth of the soldier who is being forced to remove him, and the truth of the Egyptian who wants back that patch of desert, are all three different truths. There is no truth. There's only news. But, on the air, it is most important that we be fair."[6]

Journalism has always been concerned with the competition among contesting truths, and in reporting on energy or other economic topics, the model for news people is the same: take no one side, and give the facts fairly. Yet the concepts of fairness and balance in journalism were developed in an earlier age, when scientific evidence was not so often hauled into political arguments. It has been said that "journalism is the raw material of history," which assumes that the job of analysis happens long after the newsman has completed his task. Does today's journalist, dealing with complex issues of economics or life-and-death issues of safety, march under some different banner from that of his predecessors?

JAMES C. TANNER: We should first of all separate news from views. In the editorial page of any publication are its opinions—which are not a fair and objective analysis of the situation. That publication is trying to exert influence on public opinion. But if we are not talking about that editorial page, or about something labelled "commentary" in a broadcast, or if it's not an out-and-out views publication like some represented here, then what we're talking about is a free flow of information, a fair presentation of the facts. On the *Wall Street Journal*, we used to have what we called a "however-graph," in which we always gave a so-called minority view.

DAVID KELLEY: I'd like to complicate that somewhat. I think this distinction between news and views, between reporting and expression of policy, is basically a valid one, but there is reason to have a diversity of opinion represented among those who deliver the news, in order to maintain the distinction. The problem is that you've given the relations between the two in a very obvious way. Speaking of the *Wall Street Journal*, there was an article I saw there a few weeks ago where the *Journal* had sent its people out to talk with people in business about the effects of regulation. But the reporters spoke — at least to judge by the story — entirely to people who were in business and who were living with the regulations. There was no sign that any attempt had been made to talk with people who were no longer in that business, who hadn't been able to live with those regulations. I don't think there was any straightforward bias in that story, but there are all kinds of subtle ways in which your conception of what facts are relevant to a given issue is going to decide what facts get into a purely objective, purely news story.

NORMAN MACRAE: I hate to be unpopular, but I think this is basically an American myth. What's happened in Europe is that television basically gives the news, and in the next day's national papers, they put more and more views in with the information. The classical one is the *Guardian*, which was born on the argument that "comment is free, facts are sacred." (I think what C.P. Scott really said was "comment is free and facts are too damned expensive.") American journalists are brought up with this sort of C.P. Scott belief, with the idea that there is hard reporting of news stuff. But on the great issues, I find there is really less and less hard reporting — I honestly believe you pick out which bias you're taking. I have a bias, as I pointed out earlier, toward figures, and toward modernity, or progress, if you will. Another paper taking another view would have its own biases. But when we are saying, "Oh, no, no! Hard News!," we're living in the 1920s almost.

ANTHONY J. PARISI: I would agree. Not only do I think it's a myth, but I question whether it really should, in fact, be the goal. I think I would draw the distinction between, on the one hand, objective and subjective reporting, and on the other hand, fair and unfair reporting. It's entirely possible, I think, to be subjective but fair.

MICHEL ANFROL: I think we should question at this point what is called the Fairness Doctrine in the United States, where coverage of the minority view is required. I think this kind of "balance" can lead to real distortion of the popularity of certain issues. Take, for example, the coverage of what happened in Japan regarding the Narita airport. Their only coverage in the world press was the sound of people demonstrating against the airport, and almost nothing about the millions of people who badly needed that new national airport.

WILLIAM D. SMITH: I think what we sometimes wind up doing is reporting a minority view and giving it majority status. You balance the story 50-50, even though everyone, including the reporter, knows darn well this person represents a very small minority. For example: there's a group in Washington known as Energy Action. They're noted by some quite objective and quite anti-oil people as being pretty irresponsible and slanted. But it's very hard to have an energy story without Energy Action appearing. The classic example was when the Justice Department and the FTC were studying the oil industry for possible shenanigans. At that time Energy Action was quoted as saying, "Boy, it's about time, wonderful, these guys are crooks." But when the studies were completed, totally exonerating the energy industry, Energy Action got as much space as the exoneration. Now that's giving the little guy more than his due—and I think that happens frequently, in both television and the print media. It's done for the best of reasons, but it winds up exaggerating the importance of the opposition.

JOHN F. O'LEARY: May I add a footnote to that? The then head of Energy Action, James Flug, appeared in opposition to a prospective officer of the Department of Energy some time back, and he was asked by the chairman of the committee (an unfriendly sort) who he represented. And he said, "I represent the consumers of this country." And the chairman said, "Oh, do they pay you?" And Flug said, "No, but I represent them." The chairman then asked, "Would you give me some of their names?" to which Flug replied, "Well, really, it isn't that sort of relationship." And the chairman finally backed him down to where he had four prominent Californians, a real estate operator, an oil man, and an actor who bankrolled his entire operation, which was getting essentially equal time with everyone else on any energy question in Washington.

DAVID KELLEY: One additional point about this subject. It's an important historical fact that in the '60s and '70s there's been a massive ideological, cultural change in Western societies. Things that had never been questioned before—technological progress, material progress, even the validity of science—were called into question by a whole range of people, and although those points of view aren't new anymore, they're still around, still being taught. I teach college, and all my students now take for granted a lot of what was extraordinarily controversial in the '50s or early '60s. So there's a process here that we have to keep in mind, a continuing sort of synthesis.

When a movement, an issue like that begins, I think it tends to be reported as "Here's this controversy, here are these people—they may be a little flaky but they're making a lot of noise, and we'll report them." The longer that goes on, the more that becomes a point of view which has to be represented. And it builds from there.

I think at the moment in the U.S., for example, the media people feel that environmentalists and anti-technology spokesmen have to be included because of balance considerations. If someday, anarchism becomes a widespread issue, I'm sure that reporting will have to include an anarchist's point of view, too.

Notes

1. Leonard J. Theberge, ed., *TV Coverage of the Oil Crises: How Well Was the Public Served?* (The Media Institute, Washington DC 1982), p. xi–xii.
2. S. Robert Lichter and Stanley Rothman, "Media and Business Elites," *Public Opinion*, October/November 1981, p. 42.
3. Herbert J. Gans, *Deciding What's News*, (New York: Random House, Inc., 1979) pp. 238–239.
4. Daniel Yergin, "No Quick Fix," *Columbia Journalism Review*, September/October 1979, p. 44.
5. Walter Lippmann, *Public Opinion*, (New York: Penguin, 1946) p. 8.
6. Advertisement, *New York Times*, April 19, 1982.

Index